Caring from the Heart

The Convergence of Caring and Spirituality

Edited by
M. Simone Roach, C.S.M.

PAULIST PRESS
New York/Mahwah, N.J.

Cover design by Tom Dove, C.S.P.

Library of Congress Cataloging-in-Publication Data

Caring from the heart : the convergence of caring and spirituality / edited by M. Simone Roach.
    p.   cm.
    Includes bibliographical references.
    ISBN 0-8091-3717-8 (alk. paper)
    1. Medicine—Religious aspects—Christianity. 2. Nursing—Religious aspects—Christianity. 3. Social service—Religious aspects—Christianity. 4. Caring—Religious aspects—Christianity. I. Roach, M. Simone (Mary Simone), 1922- .
BT732.C37 1997
261.8′321—dc21   97-12485
                                            CIP

Published by Paulist Press
997 Macarthur Boulevard
Mahwah, New Jersey 07430

Printed and bound in the
United States of America

Contents

CONTRIBUTORS vii

FOREWORD 1
  Ronald A. Mercier, S.J.

ACKNOWLEDGMENTS 4

PREFACE 5
  M. Simone Roach, C.S.M.

REFLECTIONS ON THE THEME 7
  M. Simone Roach, C.S.M.

ILLUMINATING SPIRITUALITY IN THE CLASSROOM . . 21
  Anne Boykin
  Marilyn E. Parker

A QUEST FOR HEALTH 34
  Nassif J. Cannon

HEALING THE FRACTURED SELF 50
  Mary-Therese B. Dombeck

CARING, SPIRITUALITY AND SUFFERING 68
  Katie Eriksson

PHOTOGRAPHY AND MUSIC GIVE EXPRESSION TO
CARING FROM THE HEART 85
  Kathryn Louise Gramling

TRANSCULTURAL SPIRITUALITY:
A COMPARATIVE CARE AND HEALTH FOCUS 99
  Madeleine Leininger

THE SPIRITUALITY OF CARING: TRANSFORMATION
TO A PARTICIPATORY CONSCIOUSNESS 119
  M. Patrice McCarthy

HOW SPIRITUALITY TRANSFORMS
THE CARE OF OLDER PERSONS 135
    Cheryl A. McCulloch

WALK IN BEAUTY: AESTHETICS, CARING
AND SPIRITUALITY 149
    Carol Picard

ILLUMINATING THE MEANING OF CARING:
UNFOLDING THE SACRED ART OF DIVINE LOVE 163
    Marilyn A. Ray

THE CONVERGENCE OF CARING
AND SPIRITUALITY: GANDHI, AN EXEMPLAR 179
    Sarla Sethi

DEVELOPING SPIRITUAL CARE:
THE SEARCH FOR SELF 196
    Gwen Sherwood

DEDICATION

*This work is dedicated to colleagues
throughout the world
who know the need for care and who,
despite innumerable obstacles, human and material,
commit themselves to teach,
practice and study better ways
to heal the wounds and brokenness
of individuals and societies,
and show by their example that it is possible
to build a caring community.*

Contributors

Anne Boykin, R.N., Ph.D., is dean and professor, College of Nursing, Florida Atlantic University. She is the immediate past president of the International Association of Human Caring and coauthor of *Nursing as Caring: Model for Transforming Practice.* Her research, scholarly writing and consultation have been in the areas of caring, spirituality and reflective practice.

Nass Cannon, M.D., blends his interest in medicine with his quest for spiritual growth, perceiving health as union with God and contributes articles on healing and integrative health for such journals as *Humane Medicine.* An internist and infectious disease specialist, Nass provides primary and consultative care and teaches at a county hospital serving the indigent. Married with three children, he views his main mission as gazing at the human heart and the human condition from the perspective of gazing at God. He hopes some healing will follow his gaze. His simple ambition is to ignite a spark of love within himself and others.

Mary-Therese Dombeck is a certified nurse clinical specialist with preparation in psychiatric/mental health nursing, theology and social anthropology. A member of the faculty of the University of Rochester School of Nursing, she practices psychotherapy, and nursing consultation at the Samaritan Pastoral Counseling Center in Rochester, New York. Her research interests are in spiritual, social and ethical issues in health care.

Katie Eriksson, R.N., Ph.D., is professor and dean, Department of Caring Science, Faculty of Social and Caring Sciences, Abo Akademi University, Vasa, Finland; professor of Nursing Science, University of Helsinki; leading head nurse, Helsinki University Central Hospital; and former dean of Helsinki Swedish School of Nursing. She is a member of the Board of the International Association of Human Caring. A leader in Europe in caring theory, her research and publications have been in the area of human caring, spirituality and suffering.

Kathryn L. Gramling, R.N., M.S.N., is a nurse-educator presently teaching at Boston College, and a doctoral student in nursing at the University of Colorado in Denver. She has practiced nursing for thirty years in service and education, with particular interest in the treatment of the adult in acute care settings. She has two sons and lives in Holden, Massachusetts with her husband.

Madeleine Leininger, R.N., C.T.N., Ph.D., D.S., Ph.DNSC., F.A.A.N., is professor emerita of nursing and anthropology, Wayne State University, Colleges of Nursing. Founder of transcultural nursing and leader in human care theory and research, she is a nationally and transnationally known educator, author, theorist, administrator, researcher and consultant, and is frequently sought after as a speaker worldwide. She established transcultural nursing as a formal field of study and practice in the mid fifties, and the International Association of Human Care in 1978. She was dean and professor of nursing at the Universities of Washington and Utah (1969–1980), and director of the centers of nursing and health research at Utah and Wayne State Universities. Author and editor of twenty-seven books and two hundred articles, chapters and films; she has done extensive field research in several western and nonwestern cultures, and was a leader in the development of qualitative research methods.

Ronald A. Mercier, S.J., a member of the New England Province of the Society of Jesus, is a moral theologian who has also done graduate studies in Russian at Harvard University. He is dean of studies at Regis College in Toronto, and is frequently involved as a lecturer in conferences and workshops in ethics, spiritual direction and retreat work.

M. Patrice McCarthy is an assistant professor of nursing at The Ohio State University, Columbus. A graduate of the University of Colorado, her work on the spiritual foundations of caring for personal and communal growth is based on Bruteau's philosophy of spirituality. She is currently involved in research, exploring the spiritual dimensions of women's experience with infertility, and feminist analysis of the social dynamics which contribute to this health crisis.

Cheryl McCulloch R.N., Ph.D., is director of nursing practice and clinical nurse specialist-gerontology at Scarborough Salvation Army Grace Hospital, Scarborough, Ontario, and an associate clinical professor, faculty of nursing, University of Toronto.

Marilyn Parker, R.N., Ph.D., is professor and associate dean, College of Nursing, Florida Atlantic University. She is principal investigator of the FAU Community-Based Nursing Project to demonstrate integration of nursing practice, education, research and development. Her research and publications emphasize art aesthetics in nursing. She is known for her publications and consultation in nursing theories, and their use in practice and education.

Carol Picard, R.N., M.S., an associate professor of nursing at Fitchburg Stage College in Massachusetts, is presently a doctoral student at Boston College. A poet and modern dancer, her research areas of interest are the use of humanities in nursing education, and aesthetics and movement as healing modalities with persons experiencing loss and life-threatening illness. She is active in international nursing efforts, lecturing at the Moscow Medical Academy and presenting frequently on international collaboration.

Marilyn A. Ray, R.N., Ph.D., C.T.N., C.N.A.A., professor, Florida Atlantic University, Boca Raton, Florida, formerly held the Christine E. Lynn Eminent Scholar Chair in Nursing, Florida Atlantic University, and in 1994–1995 was Yingling Visiting Scholar at Virginia Commonwealth University School of Nursing, Richmond, Virginia. As a certified transcultural nurse and a certified nursing administrative consultant, she has completed research on the study of caring in organizational cultures and teaches courses in human caring, transcultural nursing, nursing administration and advanced qualitative research methods. Her publications reflect interest in these areas, and she is in the process of developing and writing new methodologies related to caring inquiry.

Sarla Sethi, R.N., Ph.D., mother of two grown children—a daughter and a son—has been with the Faculty of Nursing, University of Calgary since 1970, with teaching and practice in the area of maternal-child nursing, community health nursing and transcultural nursing. Her educational experiences have been in Delhi University, India, the U.S.A. and Canada.

Gwen Sherwood, R.N., Ph.D., has had extensive opportunity to study the field of caring in nursing, pursuing qualitative research projects, scholarly inquiry and in-depth discourse with leading theorists. A frequent speaker, both nationally and internationally, she is recognized for her ability to relate theoretical concepts of caring to the practical world of the nurse, and has been named a Distinguished Lecturer since 1991 by Sigma Theta Tau International. Her publications can be found in nursing journals and in caring books published by the International Association for Human Caring and the National League for Nursing.

Foreword

Ronald A. Mercier, S.J.

The current discussions arising from the many attempts to change laws regulating euthanasia frequently resolve into debates about a little understood, but universally praised reality, interpersonal care. Whether one turns to the arguments of proponents of a change in the status quo or to the arguments that favor current limits, ubiquitous references to the appropriate care we owe each other rise quickly to the surface. This reality demands attention.

Equally importantly, however, one cannot help but note the ways in which the dialogue on "care" normally resolves into a dialogue of the deaf. Behind every presentation lurks strong, though usually implicit, assumptions about the most apt meaning for this term. Unfortunately, these assumptions tend to take the forms of *a priori* truths, unquestioned and unquestionable. What could and should be a key mode of entry into the debate resolves instead into intractable opposition.

Must this be so? Must the question of care simply be an ultimately individual, and therefore relative, one? Were that to be true, an increasing number of critical issues in our society would spin out of the realm of moral discussion and into that of private right. It would be, essentially, the death of the ethical, at least in terms of the common spaces we occupy.

Yet, parallelling the rise of recent debates on the limits of rights, based on some sense of care, a new and challenging reflection has arisen, and from a normally quiet but very competent source. As members of the health care profession have struggled to understand the meaning of their own identity as caregivers, they have had both to construct and test models of care. The results of this reflection emerge as rich and solid at the same time,

1

rich in a variety of insights and leads to follow, solid in the ways in which they help highlight realities of human life normally left unstated. The reflections of nurses, who have such intimate contact with patients and their world of relationships, have played a particularly important role in such reflection.

The authors of the current volume, themselves mostly nurses, bring the many fruits of their reflection to the question of what authentic caregiving means today. They do so from a critically needed perspective, a phenomenology of care. Within this volume, one will find a profound wealth of insight into the meaning of care, always based in solid experience. The ability to draw upon such concrete examples of care provides the reader with many and varied points of entry into the ubiquitous reality of care.

Yet, as Kathryn Louise Gramling notes in her contribution to this volume, "[c]aring is inconspicuous. As such it is devalued and threatened." Caring, because it surfaces so naturally, rarely evokes the attention needed to see its value. Only in its absence does one recognize the extraordinary value of care and its impact on our lives. The phenomenology of care in which these writers engage highlights this most profoundly human of experiences and challenges the reader to chart his/her own path of reflection.

The interdisciplinary approach which these authors utilize facilitates such an engagement. The wealth of this volume in many ways consists precisely in the varied means of reflection suggested through the example of these caregivers. Questions of spirituality, aesthetics, creativity, cultural awareness—all spring as if naturally from the pens of these contributors. They serve to challenge the dominant, functional reading of "medical care" which so often occupies our discourse and blocks out the more foundational concerns, the ones which touch us most profoundly. By no means do these authors devalue the functional or technological dimensions of such care; on the contrary, they provide a context within which to understand such means and, more importantly, the persons who make use of techniques and technologies. No one can read these reflections without knowing the "touch" which opens up our own minds and hearts, something increasingly needed in the face of our contemporary technical challenges.

Indeed, the strong and consistent concern to develop an ontology of care, a way of understanding ourselves not simply as doers or thinkers but as persons of care, provides a critically important unity to the book as a whole. Through the prism of the ties which bind us one to another, these authors open new vistas on ethical thought in our age, beyond narrow "rights" or "duties" language. From the perspective of religious ethics, their emphasis on caring links directly to the emerging discussion of the role of holiness in the moral life. The practical holiness of caring sketched out by these writers unites spirituality and ethics in a most passionate and reflective way.

As one might suspect, this volume represents only a first step in a long-term project of reflection, one which will involve both practitioners and theorists. The value of this volume may well be that it opens up the way for such a project with a most valuable contribution. To engage this volume is to be led into the path these authors have blazed; one should not be surprised that it will lead the reader, like the authors, in new and surprising directions. Such seems the very ontology of care, creative not only of new modes of treatment, but of persons moved to care and aware of its implications. We need nothing more urgently in our own age.

Acknowledgments

This work would not have been possible had it not been for the many persons who study, teach and model human caring, and most importantly, witness to its practice in their professional and personal lives. Each contributor to this volume spontaneously responded to an invitation to share their lived experience with others. Ronald Mercier, S.J., consented to do the Foreword, taking time from his demanding role as Dean at Regis College, and from a hectic schedule of teaching. I owe each of them a debt of gratitude.

From the first contact with Paulist Press, there was immediate interest. The encouragement and support of Lawrence Boadt, C.S.P., and the courteous response of staff made this work a pleasant task, and kept its conclusion always on the horizon.

Recognition is also due the Canadian Hospital Association Press, and to Eleanor Sawyer, Editor-in-Chief, who gave permission to cite from my former work, *The Human Act of Caring: A Blueprint for the Health Professions*. This work was referenced throughout the volume by many of its contributors.

The support provided by the faculty, seminarians, and staff of St. Augustine's Seminary, Toronto has been incalculable; the space, environment and resources ideal for writing. As always, living in a warm Martha community here at St. Augustine's facilitated uninterrupted progress in my research; and the affirmation of my Congregation, the Sisters of St. Martha of Antigonish, Nova Scotia, has made it possible for me to develop and use my gifts for a ministry that is not always easy to quantify. Finally, eternity will not be long enough for me to thank God for gifting me with parents who valued religious and educational opportunities, and for the guidance of Providence in my personal and professional journey so enriched by relationships with caring persons all over the world.

Preface

M. Simone Roach, C.S.M.

The reflections in this work are not primarily about nurses; nor are they exclusively about persons in health care. The authors, addressing a more fundamental level of human relationships, speak to the heart of all persons. Parents, spouses, children, colleagues, and certainly professional caregivers, live within families and communities where the give and take of human relationships shape growth and facilitate healing. We are our sister's and brother's keepers and, made in the image and likeness of God, our share in divine love enables us to love one another.

Caring from the heart is a response from the core of each person, a response to the call to be human. It is revealed uniquely in the established patterns of different cultures and manifested by all who share a common human journey. It is expressed in heroic ways in the lives of persons exemplified, for example, in Mahatma Gandhi, whose life was grounded in a praxis of justice and love, not only for the oppressed, but for the oppressor as well. Caring is made visible in the relationships of doctor and patient, as one human being facilitates the healing of another who has been violated and outraged. Caring is known through the spiritual nourishment of aesthetic experience; it is expressed and made visible through music and art. It is illuminated in an educational environment where a human caring model is primary; it is taught in response to a hunger for spirituality in the educational aspirations of students and faculty alike.

In this book, academics, researchers and teachers tell their stories. Reflecting from their experiences as caregivers, they also tell the stories of all of us; they speak for many who do not have the time or opportunity to commit their own experiences to

5

writing. Time and space do not allow for many other exemplars that could be added.

The work provides material for reflection and study, hopefully motivating the reader to examine the caring dimensions of his or her own personal and professional lifestyle. It is also intended to nurture intellectual inquiry, to provide food for thought for both student and teacher, and material for those who simply read for inspiration.

In each chapter authors attempt to show the convergence between caring and spirituality. While human caring can be demonstrated in numerous ways, spirituality is less amenable to description. Spirituality is experienced in a grasp of the sacred, the transcendent, the absolute, often expressed in the mystical; it is being alive with a sense of God. But spirituality is more than this abstract, mystical experience. Spirituality is praxis, reflecting on and responding to the gifts and woundedness of others, making the world a better place in which to live. Each writer addresses this challenge.

People in organized human services everywhere are experiencing the pressures of downsizing, of major structural changes, of alternating corporate styles, of radical shifts in management in response to financial deficits and government priorities. In the face of these pressures, it is more important than ever that we not lose sight of the core of human service, that we not fall into the trap of economic and technological expediency.

The human person is not a problem to be solved, but a mystery to be contemplated. May the reflections in this book move both writer and reader to find creative ways to understand and express human caring as we penetrate the web of interconnectedness on our rapidly shrinking planet.

Reflections on the Theme

M. Simone Roach, C.S.M.

> I looked after a man whose address was the bus shack out-
> side the mall hotel. I sat there and I held his hand and I
> watched him die, through the whole night. It was Saturday
> night and I thought to myself, this is a very strange job I
> have. You know, you're looking outside and seeing the stars
> and you know people are out and it's Saturday night and I'm
> sitting there holding a man's hand...because he's going to
> die. He has nobody to be with him when he dies. It made me
> feel very rewarded. I felt in some ways pleased that I could
> be with him. He did not have to be alone. He opened his
> eyes occasionally and he knew someone was there and I held
> his hand. (Fenton-Comack, 1987, p. 195)

The above exemplar was shared by a nurse working in a critical
care unit of a large tertiary-care, teaching hospital in the down-
town core of a Canadian city. She was involved in a research
study exploring ethical issues in critical care nursing. The nurse
shared this exemplar because, reflecting on the experiences that
evoked in her an ethical response, this one surfaced easily in her
mind. It was an experience she did not forget.

I suspect this was not a singular experience for the nurse;
she most likely provided the same quality of care to other
patients in the past. Neither do I conclude that the experience
reflected a way of caring unique to this one nurse; it is demonstrated by many other caregivers in hidden, unrecognized and
often taken-for-granted ways. On a daily basis, parents and professional caregivers alike transcend their own needs and prefer-
ences to care for others. Caring is the human mode of being.

The exemplar cited here is not a dramatic one; it does
not involve elements of the exotic ethical problems that make

7

headlines. We do not hear of an ethics committee calling family members together to discuss appropriate treatment decisions for this patient; there is no apparent concern about treatment protocol. The patient involved is simply a human being in a singularly vulnerable state, with no known source of support. He has no family member or significant other to share his pain, no one to mourn his loss when he dies. Should there be an entry in the obituary page of the provincial newspaper, and this is hardly likely, it might only read, "Mr. X, a transient with no known relatives, died at the City Centre after an illness of undetermined origin."

But there is something sacred about the bedside scene of this patient. As a unique, unrepeatable human being who as caregivers we are culturally conditioned to believe is of incalculable worth, this man represents humanity at its neediest, and calls forth from the nurse a special but natural human quality. She cares for him until he dies.

This nurse, in being with her patient to the end, is a delegate as it were, from the human family; and she embodies the qualities that most exemplify what we are all called to be for one another. Because she is a human being, she cares; because she is a nurse, she cares in a particular manner. In thinking and acting as nurse, caring for the patient becomes a particular art form; her particular way of caring is shaped by what has transformed her in her life experience and by what she has learned and experienced within a particular professional role.

The care extended by the nurse to this dying man entails a number of specific attributes. As a human person she enters into the aloneness of her patient, a man whose address is the bus shack behind the mall hotel; she is present to him in his vulnerability, responding to his condition of abandonment. She becomes a surrogate for the daughters, sons, grandchildren, friends and relatives who may not even know where father, brother, grandfather has been for many years. This nurse recognizes in the patient a human person, gives him a name and thus his dignity. Whatever the experiences that have wounded the spirit of this man, who perhaps looks much older than his years, and have condemned him to a solitary life without the most basic of human amenities, the nurse enters into a relationship, extending human compassion.

As a professional person, the nurse also gives what is most needed at this particular point in time—her presence and her touch. She held his hand. In her story, there is no evidence of complicated nursing procedures, no high technology with endless connections to physical monitors. The nursing care is of a mode requiring an investment of another kind of energy, a spiritual connection between two human souls. This is nursing competence born of the caring, therapeutic use of self—use of self as healer.

Being "present to" also elicits a response of trust from the patient. He knows the nurse is there. While not entering into a process of ethical discernment, she is drawn to be there, and to remain with the patient until he dies. This was a moral moment for her and one that, upon reflection, she humbly shared with the researcher. This beautiful story of one human being caring for another illustrates the human attribute of commitment, commitment to "promises made" by virtue of the nurse's professional choice.

A simple, but momentous life event in the journey of a dying man in the critical care unit of a large inner city hospital, becomes for this nurse, for all caregivers, and for all of us, an *exemplar*. But it is not *just* an exemplar. Rather it attests to a fundamental insight about human caring; it instills in the caregiver a sense of fulfillment as conveyed in the nurse's account, "I felt in some ways pleased that I could be with him."

This story also provides a hint of spiritual identity and spiritual connectedness between human persons, a factor which became visible within the relationship of two apparent strangers. This man could have been cared for in the luxury of a grand estate with attendants around the clock, provided with every mark of human and material comfort. The essential difference between this and the situation of our patient in the critical care unit, however, may have been experienced more by those in attendance than by the patient himself. In both instances, the most essential need of the patient was met. In both instances the need was for the presence of another human being, the healing of a touch, the warmth of concern and fidelity. In both instances the patient, to the extent he was aware, knew the reality of promise keeping. Someone was looking after him; being a companion to him during this most important stage of his life's journey.

A number of years ago, I had the privilege of being present with a dying woman and her family in India. Lying on what appeared to be a mat in a humble, makeshift shack, part of a large compound of poor people at the edge of the Arabian Sea, this woman was in the last stages of her life. While burning with fever, she had no water available even to moisten her lips. The atmosphere within the shack revealed, however, a presence that touched the depths of my soul and raised within me a stark comparison between this scene and the environment of people dying in aseptic, intensive care units in our western system of health care. While I grieved over the lack of basic material comforts available to this dying woman in India, I was moved by what I witnessed; and became aware of the power this community of persons had to transform the environment of the most modern of critical care units. One could feel the sacredness of space of this dying woman, and the spiritual bond between her and those present to her. This scene I shall never forget.

In the human encounter described in the exemplar used above, the nurse, caring for a dying man, goes beyond herself and establishes a bond with him—another human being. And this moment of transcendence is not without its demands. She reflects, "It was Saturday night and I thought to myself, this is a very strange job I have. You know, you're looking outside and seeing the stars and you know people are out and it's Saturday night and I am sitting there holding a man's hand." It seems obvious this nurse had other options. She could have left the unit at the end of her scheduled time and joined her own family and friends. What does this exemplar tell us about caring and spirituality, about caring from the heart? Does it not reveal to us how wonderfully we are made, and what potential we have for going beyond the surface of the mundane, the programmed demands of our daily routines? This exemplar catches us unaware, momentarily reminding us that we are more than what we do, that our capacity to enter into the experience of the other, to heal the broken spaces in the life of a victim of rejection and abandonment, far outweighs and goes beyond personal and communal woundedness and selfish wants.

Caring and Spirituality

Spirituality is an expression of the human person's endless search for the transcendent, a movement beyond the self. In the Judeo-Christian tradition, this is reflected in a call to relationship, a relationship initiated by the God of the promise. For all people of whatever faith persuasion, spirituality is an integral, holistic, dynamic force in human life, for the individual and for the community, and it has become a kind of universal code word for the search for meaning. Spirituality is this "something" in secular society that is being rediscovered as a lost dimension in a largely materialist world (King, 1992). One writer, Puls (1993), refers to spirituality as "a movement into *relationship,* a relationship entirely dependent on those who influence us, those who journey with us" (p. 6). In a nursing study, Paulette Burns (1991) describes spirituality as "the process of striving for and/or being infused with the reality of the interconnectedness among the self, other human beings, and the Infinite, that occurs during a depth experience" (p. 149). McCarthy (1992), in her relational ontology, shows how the spiritual dimension of human existence provides a foundation for "envisioning the fundamental relatedness of human beings and this a philosophical foundation for nursing practice envisioned as relationship" (p. 127). As Thompson (1992) notes, these themes of self-transcendence and relationahip are central to an understanding of spirituality.

> At the heart of spirituality, then, lies self-transcendence. The philosophical meaning of spirituality is that capacity for self-transcendence through knowledge and love which characterizes humans as persons. We human beings actualize this philosophical spirituality within the networks and patterns of our relationship with others. We seek meaning and are found by meaning as we interact with each other individually and in communities, and we seek truth and are found by truth in these interactions. (P. 649)

There is evidence today of a growing interest in spirituality most often translated into a search for meaning. Our search for meaning is more than a search for individual identity; it is, rather, a search for the meaning of our personhood, our interconnectedness with others. We know there is something beyond our individual, biophysical experience; we know this call within ourselves.

Caring From the Heart

This reflection on spirituality and caring moves us to a further reflection on the heart as the core, the centre of interiority, and the seat of all human activity.

The heart can be studied as an organ of circulation. In this sense, the heart is a physical structure, a vital organ, a powerful muscle on which human physiology depends. Its strength and accuracy are formidable, in some cases continuing without interruption for over a hundred years. But as wonderful and as indispensable as its organic function is for the life of a human being, rarely are physical functions used in spiritual, philosophical or psychological reflections on the human heart. As the seat of human caring, the heart is more than an organ of circulation.

The word "heart" is considered to be the most important anthropological word in Hebrew scriptures. The human heart is referred to 814 times in the Old Testament. As used in the Bible, the word "heart" refers "to the inner resources of the total person as capable of acting, with the accent more specifically on his [her] emotions: it is characteristic of Semitic thought that heart never prescinds from the total person" (Lynch, 1967, p. 965). The heart has a wide connotation in the New Testament as well. The heart denotes personality or the inner life; it is the seat of emotional states of consciousness, the seat of intellectual activities, and the seat of volition. It is thus that the divine appeal in the New Testament is addressed to the heart of the human person, the source of both good and evil.

"The important point is that, whether in the Old or New Testaments, or in rabbinic teaching, it is in the heart, in the innermost recesses of his [her] being that man [and woman] is illumined, cleansed, renewed, by attention to the word of God"

(Brandon, 1960, pp. 262-263). And this writer notes, "The heart is the source, or spring, of motives; the seat of passions; the center of the thought processes; the spring of conscience. Heart is associated with what is now meant by the cognitive, affective and volitional elements of personal life" (p. 262).

The heart, as the center for decision, obedience, devotion and intentionality, represents the total human being. The heart is the primary organ of one's being; it is the center of life, the determining principle of all activities and aspirations; it embraces everything that goes to comprise what we call a "person." The heart is the ground of the soul, the core or apex of our being. It is the place where all one's moral and spiritual battles must be won. John Vanier, founder of L'Arche Communities, dedicated throughout the world to normalizing daily living for handicapped adults, reflects, "Beneath the levels of intellect, and all of the spheres of language, communication and symbol, there lies the heart, which all have in common" (Downey, 1990, p. 194).

Mary Wolff-Salin (1989) speaks of the heart as the way in which we come to our only truly deep relationships, and away from this center the human person is alienated from self and even from others. "Refusal to choose the depths, the center, the heart condemns one to wandering forever in a domain of superficiality where both one's life with God and one's human relationships become only a fraction of what they could be" (p. 67).

The Human Act of Caring

The nurse, in her ministrations to a dying man whose only address is the bus shack, who is living the most sacred and solemn moment of his life journey, is responding as a human person. While her professional role imposes a duty, intentionally chosen by her when she decided to become a nurse, there is a sense that caring is fulfilling a human need within herself. To not care is somehow to lose her being; in her caring she becomes a more authentic human being. What might have happened if this nurse did not respond the way she did on this occasion, having acquired a pattern of relating to others in both her personal and professional life according to her own wants and needs? In creating one of his characters in *Les Miserables*, Victor Hugo gives us pause for reflection. This pathetic character is Javert, the policeman.

In *Les Miserables*, Javert's character is clearly crafted in three scenes. In the first scene, Javert held captive by the rebels behind a blockade, is turned over to Jean Valjean to be "taken care of." Jean Valjean moves him outside the blockade, fires his pistol in the air, making believe he kills him, then unbinds him and lets him go free. The second scene describes Jean Valjean's successful struggle through a sewer system with an injured person on his back, only to find Javert, the policeman, waiting at the exit. Realizing he must turn himself in, Jean Valjean asks Javert's permission to deliver a message to a friend on the way to the police station. Javert grants the permission, but when Jean Valjean returns from his brief mission, he finds Javert has left. Now he is free again! The third and tragic scene shows Javert standing on the bridge over the most dangerous rapids of the River Seine. Indulging in an agonising struggle with his own conscience, Javert finally, in utter darkness and desolation, throws himself into the rapids below. All that is heard is a splash in the night.

Victor Hugo makes an observation about Javert that captures for us the impact of caring or noncaring in the life of any human being. Hugo says, "The ideal for Javert was not to be humane, grand or sublime: it was to be irreproachable, and now he had broken down" (vol. III, p. 205). In other words, Javert could only be a perfect policeman; he could tolerate neither being cared for, nor caring for someone else. He had failed miserably; he had to kill himself! In a special sense, he epitomizes for us the realization that not to care is to lose one's being.

Caring is the human mode of being. One becomes authentically human as one's capacity to care is called forth, nurtured and expressed. Caring is essential to and for human development across the life span. It has a special relationship to human dependency shown in a revealing manner in the development of an infant.

> ...the most unique aspect of human development is the total helplessness of the human infant and the uncharacteristically long period of time in which it remains floundering in this helpless state. (Gaylin, 1976, p.31)

Gaylin goes on to observe, this dependency period is "crucial to the development of the person who loves and is loveable, who has emotions and relationships, is capable of altruism and hope" (p. 32).

Caring is not an exceptional quality, nor the response of an exceptional few. Caring is the most authentic criterion of humanness. Caring is humanity at home, being real, being himself or herself. To the extent, or to the degree, one is uncaring, to that degree one is less than human. But one knows when one is noncaring; caring is most often obvious by its absence. Caring may be suppressed or its expression inhibited, but within the core of the human person, caring is indestructible. It waits to be called forth.

As the human caring capacity is called forth and developed, its expression is manifest in a plurality of ways. Human experience both challenges and shapes the parameters and quality of its expression; education structures its form according to specific role expectations. The manner in which caring is expressed by a mother or father of a family, by a doctor for patients, by a lawyer for clients, by an engineer for a specific project, by a housekeeper for domestic detail, differs; that one is caring, however, does not derive from a specific occupational or professional role. Caring is, as it were, the call to be human. One cares in a variety of ways; that we care is what we share as human beings.

One wonders what shaped the character and personalities of the nurse caring for the patient in the intensive care unit, and Javert, the policeman in Victor Hugo's *Les Miserables*. We do not know the quality of relationships and life experiences that shaped the personality and persona of the nurse. We know less about the trauma, the negative influences that crafted the character of Javert, and that propelled him toward a tragic end.

In both instances we can only assume the choices of both were not one time events, but predetermined by a whole chain of life experiences—one a liberating response born of love, the other a tragic end born of rejection and an obsession for "doing it right." Human caring is not limited to an emotional response, much less is it merely an expression of the "touchy-feely" in human relationships. Human caring includes emotions and feeling, thinking and acting. It also calls forth the spiritual power of affectivity which, in cooperation with intellect and will, responds with joy, esteem, contempt, enthusiasm, veneration, love and compassion. Human caring is a total way of being, of being in relationship. Caring, involving head, mind, intellect, will and affections, is a response from the core of the person, the human heart.

A Synthesis

Caring, as the human mode of being, is caring from the heart; caring from the core of one's being; caring as a response to one's experience of connectedness. Spirituality, the search for meaning, the all-pervasive energy source motivating human thought and action, offers a portrait of the human journey. As a natural attraction to the source of being, spirituality seeks to integrate itself, not in self-absorption or isolation, but in self-transcendence. Spirituality is more than an abstract ideal.

One writer notes, "It manifests itself in our human responses to the brokenness of our world, the threats to our planet home, the crisis points in our lives, and the pleas and plights of human beings around us" (Puls, 1993, p.2). Spirituality is a movement into relationship; spirituality manifests itself in human caring, in a healing encounter with others.

Being infused with the reality of interconnectedness, the caring relationship touches the depths of the spiritual encounter. Spirituality is actualized through the networks and patterns of our relationships with others. Spirituality is an expression of the human heart which is seized and disclosed in human caring. Just as one must be cared for, an individual must care, must seek beyond oneself to let the other grow. Thus, in its search for meaning, in its effort to go beyond the self, the human heart surrenders to human care.

Spirituality, the search for meaning, the search for the true self; and caring, the human mode of being, one's way of being in the world, are reciprocal. As one cares, one's spiritual search becomes dynamic and other-centered; as one surrenders to the challenges of the spiritual journey, one's capacity to care is nurtured. As the human capacity to care is called forth, one comes closer to the meaning of person, moving on the journey toward the true self. While challenging the counterfeit self, manifested in one's everyday pull to exclusive self-interest and isolation, human caring discloses the authentic self as a person in relationship. The manner in which one continues and lives this search, seeking fullness of life through responding to the value of persons and the created world, reflects a caring from the heart. This is a most sublime disclosure of one's spirituality.

In finding the authentic self by going beyond the self, we experience a strange paradox. Thomas Merton casts some light on this paradox through his reflections on Adam's fall. In this reflection, Merton describes Adam as passing through the center of himself, and emerging on the other side to escape from God by putting himself between himself and God (1961, p.12; see also Finley, 1978, p.34). Our search is for the real self; what we encounter is the counterfeit self, the self of unreality. We search for identity; we encounter shadows and masks, a life structured and bounded by obsessions and make-believe. The search has communal and societal dimensions as well. We are all on a journey, and we are all searching.

Thomas Keating (1987), makes this observation:

> The realization that we are suffering from a serious pathology is the point of departure for the spiritual journey. The pathology is simply this: we have come to full reflective self-consciousness without the experience of divine union. Because that crucial conviction is missing, our fragile egos desperately seek every possible means to defend ourselves from the painful and sometimes agonizing sense of alienation from our true self, God and other people. (P. v)

Instead of developing the capacity we have to relate to others with honesty, integrity and compassion, we expend tremendous energy in controlling others, in extracting more pleasures out of life, acquiring more and better symbols of security. (Javert was compulsively bound to become the perfect, irreproachable policeman.)

It probably comes as no surprise to us that our ability and availability to be healers for others depend upon our ability to heal ourselves. Healing the self involves dismantling the emotional programs built up around the trappings of the false self. These emotional programs can be altered by repeated acts, by using discipline and sometimes, professional therapy. These are all helpful in the healing process. We know, however, from personal experience that there are places within the human person that even therapy fails to touch. The depths of interior woundedness requires the healing touch of the Divine Therapist, the Spirit of God. Nouwen (1994) provides an antidote for the psychotoxins of the false self, namely, "claiming our belovedness" (class notes).

Our bodies, minds, and souls are groaning for a deep sense of belonging. The body craves touch, food and being held. The mind craves understanding, clarity and a sense of meaning. The soul searches for inner peace, joy and a deep perception of wholeness. It is important that we know in the depths of our being that we are beloved by God.

Lost in isolation, fear and sometimes deprivation, human beings experience a pervasive hunger. While the maldistribution of food and other resources is the reason for the hunger of millions, a spiritual hunger, often unnamed and undefined, has become the consuming preoccupation of the affluent peoples of the world. Over-satiated with material things, absorbed by individual wants, and conditioned by values exclusively secular, many people on this planet suffer from the vacuum of spiritual emptiness.

The remedy is to be found within each person, between persons in relationship, in tune with who one is and with what one is called to be. Persons need to respond to and from the ground of their being, to discover in that response that the well that holds the water for every human thirst is within the human heart itself.

The remedy may be seen in the everyday lives of all of us—in the fidelity of couples to one another, in the commitment of parents to the welfare of their children and in the promise keeping of persons who have chosen particular professions in order to care for others. This remedy has been modelled, demonstrated in a seemingly insignificant way, in the critical care unit of a large inner-city hospital. It happened when two strangers, one vulnerable and in need, the other in a privileged space to care, became neighbors. The man in the last stage of his journey experienced a human touch—accompaniment assuaging his loneliness. The nurse expressed a gift, natural to her—her human capacity to care. The patient was not alone; neither was the nurse who cared for him. She took the place of all humanity, of all of us whose name is CARE.

> Once when "Care" was crossing a river, she saw some clay; she thoughtfully took up a piece and began to shape it. While she was meditating on what she had made, Jupiter came by. "Care" asked him to give it spirit, and this he gladly granted. But when she wanted her name to be bestowed on it, he forbade this, and demanded that it be given his name instead. While "Care" and Jupiter were disputing, Earth arose and desired that her own name be conferred on the creature, since she had furnished it with part of her body. They asked Saturn to be their arbiter, and he made the following decision, which seemed a just one: "Since you, Jupiter, have given its spirit, you shall receive that spirit at its death; and since you, Earth, have given its body, you shall receive its body. But since "Care" first shaped this creature, she shall possess it as long as it lives. And because there is now a dispute among you as to its name, let it be called "homo," for it is made out of humus (earth). (Roman Myth, cited in May, 1969, p. 287) As a human being, one is essentially CARE—called to go beyond the self.

REFERENCES

Brandon, O. R. (1960). Heart. In *Baker's dictionary of theology* (pp. 262–63). Grand Rapids, Michigan: Baker Book House.

Burns, P. (1991). Elements of spirituality and Watson's theory of transpersonal caring: Expansion of focus. In P. L. Chinn.(Ed.) *Anthology on caring* (pp. 141–52). New York: National League for Nursing Press.

Downey, M. (1990). Region of wound and wisdom: The heart in the spirituality of Jean Vanier and L'Arche. In A. Callaghan. (Ed.). *Spiritualities of the heart.* (1990). (pp. 186–200). New York: Paulist Press.

Fenton-Comack, M. (1987). *Ethical issues in critical care: A perceptual study of nurses' attitudes, beliefs and ability to cope.* Unpublished master's thesis, University of Manitoba, Winnipeg, Manitoba, Canada.

Finley, J. (1978). *Merton's palace of nowhere: A search for God through an awareness of the true self.* Notre Dame, Indiana: Ave Maria Press.

Gaylin, W. (1976). *Caring.* New York: Alfred A. Knopf; Avon Books.

Hugo, Victor. (N.D.). *Les miserables* (Vol. 3). (Trans. unknown). New York: Thomas Nelson and Sons.

Keating, T. (1987). *The spiritual journey: A contemporary presentation of Christian growth and transformation.* (3rd ed). Colorado Springs: Contemporary Communications.

King, U. (1992). Spirituality, society and culture. *The Way Supplement* 73, (Spring), 14–23.

Lynch, W. E. (1967). Heart in the Bible. In *The new catholic encyclopedia* (p. 965). Washington, D.C.: The Catholic University of America.

May, R. (1969). *Love and will.* New York: W. W. Norton & Co.

McCarthy, M. P. (1992). *A relational ontology: The interplay of transcendence, spirituality and community.* Unpublished doctoral dissertation, University of Colorado, Denver.

Merton, T. (1961). *New seeds of contemplation.* New York: New Directions.

Nouwen, H. J. M. and Staff. (1994). Communion, community, ministry: Introduction to the spiritual life, Course lectures and materials, RGP 2237.

Puls, J. (1993). *Seek treasures in small fields.* Mystic, CT.: Twenty-third Publications.

Roach, M. S. (1991). The call to consciousness: Compassion in today's health world. In D. A. Gaut & M. M. Leininger (Eds.). *The compassionate healer.* New York: National League for Nursing Press.

———. (1992). *The human act of caring: A blueprint for the health professions.* (Rev. ed.). Ottawa: Canadian Hospital Association Press.

Thompson, W. G. (1992). Spirituality, spiritual development, and holiness. *Review For Religious* 51, 646–58.

Wolff-Salin, M. (1989). *No other light: Points of convergence in psychology and spirituality.* New York: Crossroad.

Illuminating Spirituality in the Classroom

Anne Boykin
Marilyn E. Parker

Illuminating Spirituality in the Classroom

Higher education today is buffeted by many forces. Shrinking budgets, increased political pressures and greater student demand are but few of the influences which tend to pull us away from the nature of our work. In the face of these obstacles that tend to uproot us, we need to return to those beliefs that form the bases for knowing, believing and relating. Now is a time, in spite of these challenges, to deepen our commitments to the mission and values of higher education. It is a time to rededicate ourselves to that which is most basic to each of us in higher education. In this chapter we attempt to bring to letters, dots, commas and spaces, our sense of spirituality within the context of higher education.

We find it easier to live the connections of spirituality and education in our day-to-day actions than to express in words the reality of our knowing and doing grounded in the spiritual that is so near the center of our being. Our experiences of nursing assist us in articulating our understanding of spirituality and higher education. Our shared experiences have brought us to views on essential relations of spirituality and education. We explore the concepts from our positions as members of the university community, as professors and administrators, and from our even more critical positions as members within a community of scholars in the discipline and profession of nursing. We believe the knowing derived from our experiences is important

21

to the discipline of nursing as well as to other disciplines studied in higher education.

Spirituality

Spirituality is a way of being and living. It is a dynamic, integrated and ever-present way of knowing. As a way of living, spirituality is the essence of the mystery of being whole and at the same time dynamic; being complete and always changing; being unique and individual while always being in relation. As a way of knowing, spirituality is as constant as breath, and just as often taken for granted. While it continually supplies life, we are often ignorant of its process and many times do not respond to its constant gifts. As a way of knowing, spirituality is more than facts and reasons; more than questions and searches for truth. Spirituality allows truth and beauty to be known. The passion for knowing self and knowing self in relation, for individual integrity and for joining with the other, is based in spirituality. Indeed, spirituality finds its ultimate expression in the ongoing search rather than in the goal of final truth.

Nursing

The love of nursing and the accompanying passion for searching and knowing requires spirituality for direction and fulfillment. In nursing, the model of spirituality becomes actual; the spiritual ideal becomes real—to nurse and to the one nursed—through caring. The nature of praxis as integration of theory and action is spiritual. Hope, trust, knowing and compassion are essential concepts of spirituality and of nursing as caring. The nursing view of person as whole and complete in the moment requires spiritual awareness and grounding. Nurturing and the accompanying intimacy of nursing are expressions of the ultimate values of spirituality. Nursing education for praxis requires the model and reality of the spiritual. The community and communication so necessary in nursing require a quality of both listening and enlightening that is impossible without spiritual knowing.

Higher Education

Higher education provides an avenue to continue the ongoing search for truth. The root word of *education* means "to educate or to draw out." From this definition it can be understood that one is drawing out that which is within. The root word of *professor* means "to profess or affirm beliefs." Palmer (1983) states, "The true professor is one who affirms a transcendent center of truth, a center that lies beyond our contriving, that enters history through the lives of those who profess it and brings us into community with each other and the world" (p. 113). This definition makes clear the importance of living the relationship between self and the world. Knowing requires a personal relationship between the knower and the known. Knowledge borne through such a relationship fosters a sense of connectedness and compassion.

The desire to truly understand experiences of life embraces a sense of mutuality, reciprocity and respect for other. Through compassion one is able to experience the fullness of being human. Fox (1979) offers insights into the nature of compassion as he speaks of the interdependence of all living things. He states "...to develop such an awareness implies deep study, not only of books of course, but of nature itself. It implies study as a spiritual discipline, as a means to entering more and more fully into the truth of the universe in which we live" (p. 24). Knowledge originating out of compassion draws forth the beauty and wholeness of person. Fox (1979) states that *letting be* is to "declare the holiness of all things" (p. 91). This view celebrates the person as whole or complete in the moment (Boykin and Schoenhofer, 1993). It means persons are not viewed from a perspective of deficit but from a perspective of wholeness. Boykin and Schoenhofer (1990) further state, "the intrinsic value that persons reflect and to which they respond is the sanctity of persons, an ultimate metaphysical value that suggests a correspondence between the terms 'wholeness' and 'holiness'" (p. 149). These terms connote an understanding of the transcendent nature of being human.

How can higher education foster learning born of compassion? How can higher education support more meaningful questioning in a quest for discovery of truth? How can higher education instill the relevance of a relational context for the experience of day-to-day living? The manner in which a professor plays the mediating role between the knower and the known conveys an epistemology as well as an ethic to students (Palmer, 1983). When a faculty member responds to a student's question, the response reflects the values of higher education held by the teacher. It is through this educational experience that one learns not only an approach to knowing but also to living.

Self-Discovery Grounded in Caring

Education must be concerned with self-discovery, for it is the process of self-discovery that unites self and other in existential relationships. One of the challenges of higher education is to draw forth the multiple ways of knowing which exist within the learner. Caring is purposed herein as the critical link in the epistemological chain. Caring is a way to know the wholeness of self and other, and is an ethic for being in relationship. The emerging epistemological question is, "How do I come to know self and other as caring?"

The philosopher Milton Mayeroff (1971) provides a framework for responding to this elusive question. He describes what are termed "ingredients" of caring. To us, they are manifestations of caring. These expressions include: knowing, alternating rhythms, humility, patience, courage, hope and honesty. We believe the extent to which these are integrated into an individual's living influences how one knows others and how truth is ultimately known. Elaboration on the relationship of these ingredients to spirituality in higher education follows.

Knowing, the first ingredient of caring, is complex and multidimensional. It is our experience that knowing self is requisite for knowing other and that the mutuality of caring assures continuous and mutual knowing. Progoff (1971), a founder in the field of depth psychology, writes that where spirituality is concerned "we know that the door opens inward" (p. 13). This author has designed a comprehensive and intensive process of journalling for the purpose of coming to know self (Progoff, 1983). His poems, called "Entrance Meditations," are offered to enable persons to "go to that place within ourselves from which we can reach beyond ourselves" (Progoff, 1991, p. 13). The "reach beyond ourselves" includes enhanced openness to knowing self, other and all, including the world of nature, in relation (Progoff, 1983).

Self-discovery and knowing find fulfillment in ways of aesthetic knowing. This way of knowing subsumes other ways of knowing, such as empirical and intuitive patterns of knowing. Aesthetic knowing fosters full realization of connectedness between and among persons and objects (Boykin, Parker & Schoenhofer, 1994). Illustrations of aesthetic knowing seem to transcend the particular aspects of knowing, as connections among and between ways of knowing are expressed and appreciated. Wholeness is often cited as an attribute integral with aesthetic knowing. One study of nurse-artists found that the practice of art for the nurse leads to wholeness and fulfillment. It was also shown to be a way for searching and expressing deeply held experiences and impressions (Parker, 1992). In this study nurse-artists came to know qualities of wholeness in others, and became increasingly sensitive to connections with the lives and ways of others (Parker, 1992).

The contemporary contemplative, Moore (1992), urges us to live artfully and let ordinary activities be the basis for reflection. Such living requires no rules of art nor theories of aesthetics; such living comes from our center and receives guidance from our source. It is the experience of these authors that each of us, through aesthetic knowing, is artist when we are faithful to our intention to live fully and openly. Further, aesthetic knowing links the inner being with the outer world, thus supporting connections that join persons.

Illustrations of aesthetic knowing experienced in a clay-art workshop emphasize the processes of knowing. Outcomes of aesthetic knowing include artistic living, offering presence, overcoming separateness and remembering wholeness (Parker, 1994). Just as persons who practice an art form, each of us can learn to express ourselves through aesthetic knowing and gain new knowing as our art speaks its ever new messages. Experiences with art forms involving centering, such as described by Richards (1962), and journalling following meditation (Progoff, 1983), encourage spiritual strength, leading to growing trust and confidence in self and others. There is greater caring to nurture self and an increased knowing of rightness which engenders trust and confidence in self, others and the world at large. From this trust and confidence hope springs to life.

Humility, another manifestation of caring and one of the essential conditions for being human, is inseparable from the qualities of trust and hope. Humility is an understanding that what one has, one has been given, and that truth does not reside in any one of us but in all of us. It is a way of understanding oneself and influences the knowing of others. Mayeroff (1971) believes that the person who cares is "genuinely humble in being ready and willing to learn more about the other and himself and what caring involves" (p.23). Humility involves a desire to learn from others as well as a willingness to speak our truth and yet be in constant search of truth. It means being real—understanding who one is in all of life's situations. In humility, one is open to not knowing and makes room for others and their truth. One can only be oneself to the extent one is in touch with himself/herself. Humility allows us to let be who we are. Like caring, becoming humble is an ongoing process. The greater the humility, the more one is open to knowing and discovering truth and the more open one is to trust and hope. The circle of trust, hope and humility is encouraged by practices such as centering, meditating, various forms of artistic expression and journalling.

Other requisite conditions for knowing self and others are patience and courage. From Mayeroff's (1971) perspective, patience is an active virtue. It involves a personal involvement in which we give fully of ourselves (p. 17). Living patience calls for courage, humility, and alternating rhythm to acknowledge that the lives of others are not better directed through us. Living patience implies a willingness to enlarge one's living space—giving the space needed to support the *letting be* of others. Fox (1979) calls patience the discipline of compassion. Through patience, persons are nurtured to live fully in the moment, to experience the richness of both joy and sorrow. Patience allows one to authentically live our relationships.

Spirituality and Higher Education

Caring is the link between spirituality and higher education. Our efforts in the study of nursing and caring have led to this belief. The expressions of caring described by Mayeroff (1971) provide a framework for knowing self and other as caring and self and other in relation. Following are experiences of living the complex of spirituality and caring within the context of higher education.

How could an environment be created to reflect the living of caring and spirituality in higher education? What type of environment would support understanding, appreciating and accepting the whole person? How can the learning environment be structured to support personal participation between the knower and the known, and therefore influence the knower's way of relating in the world?

Central to this discussion are basic assumptions that "caring is the human mode of being" (Roach, 1987,1992); persons are whole or complete in the moment (Boykin and Schoenhofer, 1993); and that all are interconnected. Implicit in these ideas is the belief that every person is unique and at the same time part of all other humans. Each person plays a vital role in the discovery of truth and no one thought is valued more than another. Therefore, there are no judgements. All ideas are encouraged and tolerated.

One way to portray these beliefs is through an organizational pattern which is circular. Rather than a traditional hierarchical structure which conveys values in a horizontal manner, the model of a circle reflects the importance each person plays. All persons are at the same level and there is a welcome opportunity to truly know self and other. Each learner is valued, recognized and celebrated for the gifts he/she brings. Each person supports the goals of higher education as ideas are freely shared in the search of truth. The knower co-participates with the knowledge of the moment in a community comprised of other persons. As a community, there is a discovery of the importance of understanding experience and relatedness which form a bond for living and for an ongoing search for truth.

Something as simple as the arrangement of a classroom can support the belief that the input of all persons is valued.

Organizing a room in a circle implies oneness and may disperse the image of the teacher as one who owns the knowledge and determines what knowledge is important to impart. Teacher and students can use this arrangement as a way to convey the importance of each person.

An important approach to knowing involves dialogue and participation of each knower. In order to prepare for such engagements, moments of silence are valued. Each person shares authentic thoughts and experiences and is encouraged to broaden his/her perspective in order to take in more and more of the world. Through listening to each other and entering the dialogue, there is a transformation into a sense of a larger reality. The experiences of living and relating take on new meaning; compassion grows. Caring is the central groundedness of the dialogue. It is a commitment to caring as a way of being in the world that guides what ought to be.

Would there be a difference in our teaching and learning if, as members of a discipline, the focus of study was on the search for truth? Knowing, not knowledge nor truth for its own sake, would be the purpose of our living and being. For example, the "knowing" of the discipline of nursing comes from studying situations of our practice, not from texts or personal experiences which serve to inform our knowing. It might be helpful to elaborate on how a particular approach to the study of nursing guides this search. Because nursing is a relational discipline, it is important that nursing education focus on nurturing the development of the student. In order to achieve this knowing, students study the question "Who am I as caring person?" and "How is my caring expressed to self and other?" These questions encourage knowing the wholeness of self and other. Readiness to address these questions includes deliberate attention to being quiet, preparing to listen for internal and external cues or leadings, and willingness to be present and open to possibilities. It is in this openness that one becomes more fully aware of self and more fully knowing of others.

A reflective exercise on simple words such as "stillness," "quiet" and "listening" raises to consciousness the importance of these concepts as a basis for learning, relating and forming community within the classroom. Students are asked to reflect on the meaning of these words, drawing on internal sources as well as sounds and sensations from the external environment. Such ways to know are often new to university students, and as with other new ideas, actual experiences are helpful in order to make choices about the use of silence and active listening in the future. Following the exploration of these ideas, students begin each class with two minutes of silence for a period of weeks. Many students find this thoughtful reflection and dialogue engenders a sense of group connectedness. It seems that trust and willingness to be honest are heightened within the group and that calmness rather than anxiety is the rule.

Use of the caring ingredients provides a way to explore and articulate responses to the elusive question, "Who am I as caring person?" Students respond through class dialogue or journalling to questions such as, "How do I express my humility, courage, patience and hope in day-to-day living?" A student journalled that being a beginning student of the discipline requires courage and humility. Entering nursing situations poses many unknowns: the setting, ill persons and their families, other professionals, and new technologies. Students speak about the importance of being supported in the learning process. Cited as essential are a teacher's active patience and trust that students will grow and achieve at their own rates and in their unique ways. One student, when asked at the end of a course about the experience of coming to know self as caring person, stated:

> I feel that I'm perched upon a lily pad in this vast sea of life...My trip to the lily pad was not without struggle...My confidence increased when I realized that each lily pad was unique in its own...How could I not have noticed all the wonderment around me...? My consciousness is now expanding more. I'm more open and sensitive. I take more time to see things deeper and broader. (Boykin, 1994, pp. 83-84)

The content of nursing is discovered through the shared study of lived experiences of nursing praxis we call nursing situations. Each nursing situation is unique, whole and dynamic. Multiple ways of knowing are used to study each nursing situation which brings forth an integration of nursing and related theory and research. The following aesthetic expression of a nursing situation has been used to study nursing.

Love Is a Small Spoon

I look at a tiny frame 93 years of age, (and much less in pounds) curled up in the same position as in the womb, and I wonder, dear Lord...what goes through her mind?
She's unable to speak, and so weak she can hardly move.
She DEPENDS
on those of us around her
to meet her needs.
She gets something to drink when I offer it,
something to eat when I feed her.
She gets turned when I turn her
bathed when I wash her.
Ah, yes, she DEPENDS, Lord,
on those of us around her.
She's fortunate, this little lady, that those who tend to her needs really love her. I've been told she loves mashed potatoes and hates spinach...and told definitely to use a small spoon, please!

This frail frame, almost lost in the bed sheets, will only be with us for a short while...then she'll be back at the nursing home with those who know about small spoon and mashed potatoes.

But I still wonder what goes through her mind? Does she pray? Does she talk with You, Lord? She'll have to DEPEND on You, oh Lord, for You are around her more than anyone. I know she'll do fine...because You know all about mashed potatoes and small spoons...but more importantly,

You know how to nourish her and are for her, and give what she needs most!

All this reminds me dear Lord, of how I must DEPEND on You for my needs!

You feed me with the Eucharist and Your Scripture...(much better than mashed potatoes).

I thank You Lord,
for feeding me when You choose...and not giving me
    spinach too often.
I thank You Lord, for allowing me just to be
still...curled up under the sheets when I need to
rest...and waiting for You to "move me."
I thank you, most of all Lord
for that loving touch...that knows the unique me so well;
that knows how to feed me with a small spoon!
I am truly grateful...
Bless my 93 year old patient, Lord.
Bless me...(Oetting, 1991)

Students are guided in the study of nursing using this or another nursing situation. The dialogue is guided by several related questions: (1) Who is the nurse as caring person? (2) Who is the older woman as caring person? (3) What are hopes of each person for living caring in the moment? (4) How can the wholeness of the situation best be described? (5) What calls for caring are experienced by the nurse? (6) What are nursing responses in the illustration? (7) What are other calls for caring and other nursing responses? (8) What are hoped for outcomes in the nursing situation? (9) What knowing from nursing and related disciplines of knowledge assists in understanding this nursing situation? (10) In what special ways might this nursing situation serve to inform nursing situations of the future? As students engage in answering these questions, a wide range of nursing responses are brought forth and the uniqueness of nursing practice is revealed. Responses to these and other questions occurring in the teaching-learning dialogue illustrate the freshness and uniqueness of each nursing situation. Nursing situations serve as a way to know wholeness; to experience connectedness; and to integrate and appreciate multiple ways of knowing.

A student enrolled in a nursing course concerned with studying nursing in acute settings with parents and children, wrote the following poem as an expression of her nursing situation:

Born too soon
I lay in this artificial womb you've created
and wait for your touch.

I feel like broken glass as I lay here
surrounded by the sound of the machines I need.
The flashing light keeps me company as I wait for you.
I sleep as life-giving fluids drip in my veins
and still I wait.
I live for your touch. That's when I feel most alive!
Are you my mother?
I don't know but I love you and know that love
is returned a hundred times
as we rejoice in my progress toward life.
And every day I know that you will come and give me
your loving touch.
And when you come you touch me ever so gently, careful
so as not to dislodge the many tubes that keep me alive.
But they are nothing compared to your touch.
You hold me so softly in your hands—turning me, weighing me,
washing me, recording my progress.
And finally the moment I long for comes as you
hold my hand in yours
stroke my head
and sing a lullaby. (Dodge, 1992)

Conclusions

In this chapter the essential relationship of spirituality and higher education is presented as expressed through the discipline of nursing. Higher education is viewed as embracing an ongoing search for truth. This process fosters self-discovery for the learner and prepares one to receive a greater understanding of his/her reality as well as the reality of others; to develop a sense of identification, connectedness and compassion with others, and a deeper understanding of truth.

Caring provides the framework for knowing in this search. Through caring, one is able to see, hear, speak and think honestly and to relate more wholly to self and others. Caring becomes the moral basis for relating. Through the commitment to *live* caring, there is a mutual effort to provide space for knowing and speaking truth. Spirituality sustains the ongoing focus of the search.

REFERENCES

Boykin, A. (Ed.) (1994). *Living a caring-based program.* New York: National League for Nursing Press.

Boykin, A. and Schoenhofer, S.O. (Winter, 1990). Caring in nursing: Analysis of extant theory. *Nursing Science Quarterly,* 3(14), 149–55.

——. (1993). *Nursing as caring: A model for transforming practice.* New York: National League for Nursing Press.

Boykin, A., Parker, M.E., and Schoenhofer, S.O. (1994). Aesthetic knowing grounded in an explicit conception of nursing. *Nursing Science Quarterly,* 7 (4), 158–61.

Dodge, E. (1992). Born too soon. *Nightingale Songs,* 2 (2), West Palm Beach, Florida.

Fox, M. (1979). *A spirituality named compassion.* San Francisco: Harper and Row.

Mayeroff, M. (1971). *On caring.* New York: Harper and Row.

Moore, T. (1992). *Care of the soul.* New York: Harper Perennial.

Oetting, P. (1991). Love is a small spoon, *Nightingale Songs,* 1(3), 2, West Palm Beach, Florida.

Palmer, P.J. (1983). *To know as we are known: A spirituality of education.* New York: Harper and Row.

Parker, M. E. (1992). Exploring the aesthetic meaning of presence in nursing practice. In D. Gaut (Ed). *The presence of caring in nursing* (pp. 25–38). New York: National League for Nursing Press.

——. (1994). The healing art of clay. In D. Gaut and A. Boykin (Eds). *Caring as healing: Renewal through hope.* (pp. 135–45). New York: National League for Nursing Press.

Progoff, I. (1971). The star/cross: An entrance meditation. New York: *Dialogue House Library.*

——. (1983). *Life-study experiencing creative lives by the intensive journal method.* New York: Dialogue House Library.

Richards, M.C. (1962). *Centering: In pottery, poetry and the person.* Middleton, Conn. Wesleyan University Press.

Roach, S. (1992). *The human act of caring. A blue print for the health professions.* (Rev.ed.). Ottawa: Canadian Hospital Association.

A Quest for Health

Nass Cannon

This quest for health will examine the nature of health and healing and the formation of the care provider, reflect on the meaning of caring, and the relationships of care provider to care recipient in a communal context.

HEALING THE HUMAN HEART

The Wounded Patient

Often we do not take time to listen to the stories of the wounded who seek our ministering touch. Knowing their story forces us to approach them as persons who require our time and humanity rather than our objective, impersonal acts of therapy (Greiner, 1991).

Recently, an old lady exposed her wounds. Shuffling to steady her gait, the fat lady leaned on her cane, swung onto the examining table, fixed her black eyes on me, and said, "I have come to get a blood test." I assumed she wanted a serum cholesterol. Impatient with my musing, she blurted, "I want a blood test for the virus." Startled, I focused on the elderly woman who wore a loose blouse, pants, and balanced a very large abdomen that hung almost to her knees. With every movement, arthritic pain shot through dark eyes, with dilated pupils, lost in a sea of flesh. The woman snapped, "I want the AIDS test". More curious, I asked her age. "Eighty," she replied. I shyly asked why she wanted an AIDS test. She related her story.

"I live alone in a project apartment. Three weeks ago, I had a birthday. My children came to my house, brought a cake and food. People who live near me came. Some I did not know so well but have seen. After the party, I took a bath and put on my bed clothes. I went to bed to read. I heard a click in the door like a key turning. Before I could move, a young man jumped on top of me. He beat me on the head and arms, cut my lip and tore my clothes. He raped me. I want an AIDS test."

Having dealt with the reason for her visit, she cried. Violated in body, mind, soul, she sat like a lump of dough reliving the imprint of the semi-stranger who violently stamped her life with the physical, emotional, and spiritual reality of his rape.

Twice since then she returned for unrelated complaints. At each visit she told the events of her rape as though the retelling would make it go away. The man continues to live nearby. Although she changed the apartment lock, food, clothing and money disappear. She sleeps with a pistol waiting for him to return. The assault of the rapist fractures her emotions and wounds her soul. Bruised in body, mind and spirit, she possesses memories of the event that have become a preoccupation. Although her body regains its daily rhythm, the event is stamped in her memory and colors her emotions with anger, resentment and alienation. From the encounter, I relearn the essential elements of compassionate caring—listening, identifying, empathizing. Listening to her story opens me to identify and empathize with her suffering, allowing a stranger to become an acquaintance. Her story transforms her from client to person, and arouses my compassion as I empathize with this victim of a neighbor-become-rapist.

The Broken Healer

I am a physician who views his root identity as one called to heal. Yet, I experience myself as broken, as one admonished by the phrase, "Physician heal thyself." Perhaps you, too, in your healing ministry, experience yourself as a broken healer. Let us together explore some notions regarding the healer as broken, examine the nature of healing, and consider the relationship of the healer to the one healed (Cannon, 1987).

We care providers as healers share in the mortality and
brokenness of those we encounter. A few years ago my brother
had abdominal pain. His evaluation revealed gall stones, a duo-
denal ulcer and major occlusion of a coronary artery. He
received by-pass surgery, blood transfusions, and returned to
work. Several years later, his physician, evaluating fatigue, diag-
nosed chronic hepatitis caused by the blood transfusions. He
subsequently bled from distended veins necessitating a special
shunt procedure. His other illnesses included a bladder tumor,
for which he had surgery and chemotherapy, and diabetes melli-
tus, which required insulin.

In our care of such as my brother, we ponder a patient's
decline and see ourselves as though we were looking into a mirror and watching our own deterioration. We breathe sickness
and suffering, death and dying with a finger on our pulse and a
self-reflective mind awaiting our own inevitable collapse.
Recently I saw a middle-aged female whom I will call Sue, with
anxiety attacks and ischemic heart disease. Sue related that eight
months previously her husband and daughter had had an auto-
mobile accident which killed her daughter and left her husband
permanently bed bound. She adopted her daughter's only child,
who does not hear or speak, and provides care for her husband.
Sue voices frustration, weariness, anger and expresses guilt for
her occasional desire to abandon them. Because of recent rob-
beries in her neighborhood, she cannot sleep, and constantly
worries about becoming disabled.

We move through this world of sickness and suffering, not
as observers, remote and detached, but as participants, victims
among other victims; the days, the nights, become a blur of tor-
mented faces, racked bodies, confused minds—an endless stream
of suffering humanity passing by—not so much before us as with
us, as together we march toward death.

As we minister unto others, we must not be surprised at our
own capacity for betrayal and even *evil*. As broken healers, we
will find in ourselves the darkness of rage, rejection, malice,
greed, lust and pride that lurk in our interior. In our encounters,
these dark forces often surface, tempting us to injure those we
seek to heal. Also, long exposure to suffering creates a numbing

effect—an anaesthetizing of our sensibilities best classified and expressed as indifference. I recall an early morning admission during my internship when I angrily stood over a male alcoholic who was vomiting on me, and pinched his chest to wake him while I shouted epithets for his self-inflicted injury that kept me from sleep.

The recognition of these forces provides us an opportunity for humble growth. By acknowledging our weaknesses and seeking forgiveness when appropriate, we find healing as we seek to heal. Fruits of the penetration of our brokenness include compassion and a release of the spirit of healing. I will never forget the first patient we admitted to our hospital with AIDS at the beginning of the epidemic. Although our team perceived itself to be compassionate care providers, we were smug, intolerant and fearful about AIDS. We resented the demanding mother who insisted that we provide her son the care and dignity that he deserved. Mother and son exposed our brokenness, forcing us to examine our attitudes and prejudices, and acknowledge our fear. During the lengthy hospitalization, they wore at our consciences and transformed our perceptions from seeing a host with virus to a person with illness. They penetrated our psychic quarantine and opened us to compassionate caring.

Two other fruitful benefits of our brokenness as healers include the experience of sorrow and growth in tender-heartedness. As healers, we experience sorrow in our relationships with others—sorrow in our errors of judgement, sorrow in our neglect and indifference. We inhabit a world of sorrow, a world deeper than regrets or sadness, a world in touch with the aches and pains of the human heart. This pain-filled world exceeds the reaction—"I am sorry." It is deeper than that. Sorrow reflects a property of love as we suffer with them, realizing that nothing we do can change their suffering. Presupposing care and compassion, sorrow measures the depth of our love.

A virtue opposed to indifference, tender-heartedness relates to an interior stance which involves having tender feelings, but tender-heartedness transcends feelings or sympathy. Storms of anger, revulsion, frustration and even rage may arise in our encounters. Tender-heartedness indicates the will to treat others as you would have them treat you, and to encounter a human person, not a disease or a process. It pertains to the constant struggle not to let our beliefs, prejudices and feelings create barriers in our encounters. Tender-heartedness must not be misconstrued as the evasion of a hard decision, softness in the face of a necessary confrontation, the denial of emotion or retreat before the truth of physical, mental, or spiritual realities. Rather, it communicates an interior stance of openness as a friend—an I-wish-you-well attitude. A measure of the realization of our brokenness, a tender heart projects kindness, patience and compassion.

We discover that our brokenness is a precondition for healing (Nouwen, 1979). Our quest for health of mind, body and soul through the medium of God's power to heal becomes the source of healing for others—our brokenness joined to his. The power to heal explodes from the very depths of our brokenness (MacNutt, 1977). As we assent to heal one another, to care for one another, God assents to heal us, to care for us, so that in the process of healing, we find healing.

The Nature of Healing

The essence of healing surpasses the alleviation of suffering to include reconciliation or personal harmony. Genuine healing goes beyond a repair process, a replacement of spare organs or the eradication of an infectious illness. Genuine healing transcends the repairing process to include deep integration of body, mind and spirit. Healing ultimately means wholeness, a unity of body-mind-spirit. It reveals a harmony that transcends body or mind or spirit alone because, as human persons, we are neither body nor mind nor spirit, but a body-mind-spirit unity (Goodloe, 1992). Even in the face of irreversible disease or disability, this harmony manifests itself.

A friend of mine has multiple sclerosis. Over the years I have watched her mental and physical capacity wane as her spiritual capacity soared. She impatiently wishes to peak beyond the veil, to experience more complete union with God. Unlike my friend, many persons do not acknowledge their spiritual embodiment, the presence of God within them. In our society, and within the health care system itself, most of our attention extends to health of body, little to mind, and least of all to the human spirit.

There is, nonetheless, a recognition of the experience of mystery in human suffering (Starck, 1992). We may be able to kill pain with drugs, but these same drugs, as wonderful as they are, do not touch the core of suffering within the person. Suffering calls for a healing that is relational. Isaiah's account of the Suffering Servant reveals, in mystery, the heart of all healing. In his account, healing arises from a Suffering Servant whose stripes and brokenness generate healing. We, as healers, are invited to share in the brokenness of the Suffering Servant; we are invited to explore our own brokenness, to join it to his and share, too, in his power to heal. Health care, as a composite of care providers with specialized knowledge, medications, technology and procedures, ensues in a profound encounter if permeated by the spirit of the Suffering Servant.

Formation of Healers

As care providers, how do we acquire a merciful heart? In our training we acquire much skill in the technical aspects of caring but little opportunity to reflect on the origin of our desire to care. The stillness of the human heart has incubated both a Mother Teresa and an Adolph Hitler. Consider the community of hardened hearts, (brewing rage, sadism, murder,) that gave birth to the holocaust in contrast to the community of Mother Teresa birthing mercy in its service to the poor. The human heart can be filled with grace or evil; grow in wisdom and grace or folly and sin—a reality that may inflame our passions, accelerate our greed, impel us to murder our neighbor. The heart satiated by excesses of materialism, wealth and power may become hardened to the cry of those who suffer.

Our modern world abounds in such obstacles. In western society materialism, gluttony, lust, and greed have become a way of life. Our eating habits accelerate heart disease; we infect each other with deadly diseases; we consume inordinate resources; we

build disposable shopping malls while most of the world population starves. We overindulge the appetites of our bodies, fill our
minds with illusionary delights, make our hearts prisoners of our
passions. We pursue these destructive ends because our hearts
serve these attachments.

To soften our hearts as care providers some consideration
should be given to the means of conversion, the process of turning our hearts from destructive attachments to merciful concern.
The means include fasting, compunction, prayer, reconciliation
and a desire for inner healing.

Fasting liberates the body, mind and heart. The discipline
of fasting allows the mind to be open to the suffering cry.
Fasting disciplines our bodies, opens our minds for compassionate regard of our suffering neighbor and softens the heart for
compunction.

Compunction, the sorrow we experience for our heart's
inordinate attachment to things, or to the love of self, results
from the realization of our failure to love God and neighbor.
Fasting exercises our wills; compunction, as a gift of God's
mercy, exercises our hearts. Fasting softens the heart; compunction converts the heart to a love of God and neighbor.
Compunction allows us to experience God's forgiveness and
mercy, thereby freeing us to forgive ourselves and others.
Compunction schools and dilates the heart allowing the care
provider to be a channel of God's mercy (Ward, 1975).

Mercy, a fruit of compunction and the most perfect virtue
regulating the relationships of persons, manifests itself in goodness toward others. Performing the works of mercy transforms a
labor of effort and competence into a labor of joyful love (sorely
missed by many practitioners). By contrast, care providers with
values opposed to mercy may render harsh treatment and end in
the exploitation of others as commodities. As a commodity, the
other becomes someone to whom we do things rather than
someone to whom we relate; the person disappears, the three-
vessel coronary disease remains. Our institutions for healing
become mechanistic assembly lines.

The formation of a merciful heart depends upon prayer,
through which we communicate, not only with God, but with

ourselves and with our neighbor (Merton, 1971). Prayer allows the integrative power of love to propel us in health of body, mind and soul as we acquire the spiritual resources to be merciful in our relationships with others. For Christians, a reflection on the hidden life of Jesus may give insight into the meaningfulness of our lives as prayer. Before his public ministry, Jesus lived an ordinary life as a carpenter's son while remaining in loving communion with God, his Father. Assuming the Christian belief that Jesus was true man and true God, his every thought, word or deed was in communion with his Father and, therefore, prayer. His moments of solitude, when he communicated in secret with his Father, were no more or less prayer than when he worked as a carpenter. Yet he grew in wisdom and grace through the mundane realities of his everyday life. The love in him animated all that he did, and this love, the very substance of God, made God present in his every activity. Enveloping all of his moments as communion and communication with God, the entire life of Jesus signified a living prayer.

As care providers we can transform our lives into living prayer so that our interactions with the suffering become supercharged with the vitality of the presence of God. Fasting and prayer help us to accomplish the spiritual quest of integration, healing ourselves as we become ministers to others.

The process of reconciliation provides for a healing of the divisions within the self, calming our unhealthy obsessions, balancing the pursuits of body, mind and spirit into a harmony that makes for peace and allows for personal healing.

This harmony, this quest for peace and inner healing is nourished by a strong desire for health of mind and soul. Modern psychology and psychiatry have significant contributions to make to the healing of the emotions (Maher, 1993); God's grace works through these and other modalities. We need help, nonetheless, to allow ourselves to be led. The mystery of human freedom calls us to desire, to choose; the many impediments of our unruly habits and desires often stand in the way. We need the energy that comes from relationships—our relationship with God and with each other.

Care and the Care Provider

The practice of humane caring requires art, science and virtue. The art includes such elements as communication skills, a bedside manner conducive to healing relationships, intuition and a gentle touch which envelopes the science of medicine (Cannon, 1992). Important virtues include compassion, trust, generosity and integrity, always providing the care participant space, leisure and opportunity for partnership. Humane medicine must be rooted in our shared humanity; the golden rule provides guidance for equal partnership. The process of caring based on our being complimentary and refracting the image and likeness of God, elevates our encounter to communion. Communion occurs when the two of us pass beyond words and the tending of the care of the illness, to the mirroring back of the image and likeness of God to one another. While communion may occur in any encounter, it has a special and unique character in the healing relationship.

The purpose of human caring in the context of healing encounters is to facilitate growth in wholeness. Caring is the human mode of being (Roach, 1992); each human person has the capacity to care. But this capacity may lie dormant for a whole variety of reasons, rendering one unable to care and, in a sense, inhuman. One may be anti-caring, even bestial. Some of the grotesque abuses of children, the elderly, the disadvantaged, stem from a predatory anti-caring disposition mirroring a deep spiritual disorder. Brutality in all its forms may disrupt the tender roots of caring. Abused children may become abusing parents. Care providers brutalized in their training may be less than ideal communicators of care. This realization has profound implications for education (Kohn, 1991).

Teaching Caring

Particular attention should be paid in medical and other health care educational institutions to the attitudes and behavior of faculty and staff which brutalize care providers. A surgical resident, raked over the coals by his chief for some minor transgressions, was faced with the choice of spending his time being a superior surgeon at his chief's institution or tending to his wife and two children somewhere else. Students may be brutalized by the rigorous and demanding knowledge requirements, competitive examinations and alienation from faculty and supportive staff. Their experience may breed a cynical and harsh, self-centered attitude. Much of the tender roots of human caring which led them into a health care field in the first place may be uprooted by the brutality occurring in the name of competence. Because students must demonstrate a certain level of proficiency on standardised examinations, preoccupation with a large volume of information consumes most of their waking hours, leaving little time for nurturing human relationships and their connection to the humanities. The human development of the student may be delayed or suffer irretrievable damage.

The care we provide our care providers in training is of critical importance to their acquisition of care competence. Tremendous energy has been given to technological competence and procedural skills, but care competence has been largely ignored. Our educational centers should value, research and teach the art of caring (Thayer-Bacon, 1993). Above all, they must foster a caring environment where exemplary caring models are visible. This places a great but noble onus on the shoulders of presidents, deans and chairpersons in health care institutions.

One of the negative pitfalls of education within busy and crisis-oriented health care institutions today is care fatigue. While a frequent occurrence often resulting from excessive and unrealistic demands on oneself and others, care fatigue most often goes unrecognized. Signs of care fatigue may be as simple as an expression of the feeling, "If I hear one more complaint!" to a shouting match between a patient and a doctor who has been on call the night before. Recognition of these signs along with provision for breaks and occasional solitude, are important responses to the age-old, but always perennial, "Physician heal thyself."

Another difficult challenge in the everyday life of many caregivers today is care provider abuse. Provider abuse may range from a ritualistic call repeatedly made at 2:00 A.M., to physical injury or psychologically demeaning behavior on the part of the patient and/or family. A distinction must be made between patient needs and demands; care givers have not only the responsibility, but the right to establish ground rules for the professional relationships that must exist if healing is to take place.

HEALING RELATIONSHIPS

Nature of Relationships

The care provider exists in relationships. Our ability to care for others depends upon establishing and maintaining healing relationships. Relationship involves the process of intertwining of persons so that they grow in communion with one another and, though separate, create a sphere of common identity. To sustain a relationship, space, leisure and means for interaction must be available, as well as a common ground (physical, emotional or spiritual) for communication. The intensity of the relationship escalates as one moves from the physical to the emotional and spiritual. Also, the intensity of the relationship depends upon the space, time and leisure devoted to it. To establish healing relationships with our patients, we must commit the space, time and leisure that will nurture communion.

Relationships may be expressed creatively or destructively. Creative relationships manifest love, mutual healing, affirmation, and tend toward union. Mature relationships display sacrificial attributes in which another's interest equals, if not exceeds, one's own. Olivia illustrates this attribute to a heroic degree. Olivia has malignant hypertension and two strokes, yet she still serves fifty hungry people through her church ministry. Olivia shops, prepares and serves her daily meal.

Characteristics of destructive relationships include superior/inferior roles, physical, emotional and spiritual violence, egocentric behavior and victimization. Destructive relationships involve power assertions and manipulative self-seeking by one party at the expense of the other. A terrifying example of this occurred when Mary stopped to fix a flat tire. Three males feigned assistance, abducted and raped her. Locked in the bathroom, Mary escaped by breaking a window and crawling out.

Broken relationships engender hurts and disappointments which inhibit new relationships. Hence, failure in relationship becomes self-sustaining. Abused children may become abusers; children of divorced parents carry the pain of separation into their own relationships. The communal consequence of broken relationships includes societal fragmentation and dispersal. Poverty in relationships exist in a society rich in material goods. Societal division and strife originate in our impoverished relationships. Broken relationships result in lack of purpose and societal loss of unity and community. Hurt feelings and the memory of past injuries affect the vitality of one's current relationships, and injuries over a lifetime generate a storm of emotions that can explode at any moment (Linn, 1972). Wanda, suffering severe spouse abuse for twenty years, shot and killed her husband as he walked into their house with his girlfriend.

Love heals relationships, and the formation of multiple loving relationships at differing levels of intimacy—spouse, children, friends, clients—generates healing in the couple, the family, the community, and society. The individual's decision to love initiates healing relationships. The decision to love joins the human will to the Spirit of Love which enables the achievement of God's purpose for the individual, couple, community and society (van Breeman, 1974).

In the context of healing relationships, our quest for health and wholeness requires our personal conversion and repentance by letting go of our destructive ways, forgiving and forgetting, and turning toward the Source of Love.

The Healer's Relationship to Others

We, as healers, in our relationships with the suffering other, may intensify our communion. We identify and penetrate their suffering in empathetic degrees. First, through knowledge of their story, we acquire a conscious awareness of the content of their suffering. Through a sustained relationship, we immerse ourselves in the other's suffering through empathetic understanding. As our intimacy progresses, we can feel the other's pain much like we would in a loving family when a child or brother becomes ill. A final degree of involvement very rare and unique belongs to the mystical realm. Imitators of the Suffering Servant such as St. Francis of Assisi, or St. Therese, the Little Flower, voluntarily assent to suffer for others (Clarke, 1977). Somehow the vitality of their sufferings showers spiritual, mental and even physical healing upon others, even though those individuals may be unknown to them personally. This involves the concept of a mystical union whereby all of us connect to one another and affect one another, both living and dead, through the mystery of our forming one body.

Healing relationships require community because the power to heal resides in the community. It is not the property of doctors or nurses or financial managers. For that matter, it is no one individual's property. A gift that dwells collectively in the community, healing can manifest itself most forcefully when the whole community mobilizes itself to care for the suffering other. It is a communal event in the direct, supportive, healing relationships of family and friends, and in the invisible relationships of prayer and ritual. We broken healers must pay attention and listen to one another, have respect for one another's unique healing gifts, affirm them, develop them, and allow their expression (Dashiff, 1990).

In our communal ministry, we should come to listen reverently to the testimony, the witness of the suffering other. We must receive the communications of our patients as more than factual exchanges. We must listen deeply for the faint sounds of the divine spark writing us a letter of love, in the concrete humanness of our sufferers as we hear the disclosure of their story, of who and why they are, of the pains and hurts of being them. As we grow in our regard for the suffering person, we may come to feel for them as though they were our sons or daughters, our brothers or sisters. This tender regard can progress to experiencing them as our very other selves, in which we recognize our sameness without losing our individuality. And so the whole communal aspect of the healing process should be approached as a big family—this brother with cancer, this one with heart problems, this sister with leukemia, this little brother with AIDS.

Two young men with AIDS died recently. During their long difficult struggle, they came to know the heart of rejection. They lived at the center of isolation. They were perceived as biological founts of contagion, viewed with suspicion, distrust, contempt and hatred. Never have I encountered such despair as gripped these young men. The last one to die was fecal incontinent. His mother cared for him. Her family and other children shunned them. They had no money, no food, no gas. Their washing machine broke! The second one was discharged from the hospital and died at home shortly afterwards without even the spiritual consolation of his church! And where was I? A shuffling eighty-year-old lady was raped, and where were all of us as a community of concern?

Faced with the anguish of the suffering person, we must choose our response. We hope for a kind and merciful reaction, but that is not always the case. Sometimes our hearts, harboring indifference or overloaded with our many concerns, drown the cry of those who are suffering. Nonchalant, mechanistic, impersonal care may follow.

Final Thoughts

In this chapter we have reflected on healing from many perspectives. We listened to the wounded, observed the broken healers and examined the nature of healing. We proposed means for the formation of care providers and espoused the golden rule as a principle to govern caring relationships. We concluded that healthy relationships facilitate communion with God and neighbor. We suggested that growth in health, characterized by progressive integration of body, mind and spirit leads to wholeness and facilitates union with God and neighbor. The Spirit of God as love actualizes health of body, mind and spirit, and union with neighbor. Love begets both individual integration and communal unity.

Collectively, our quest for health has a communal extension. By our choices we choose either loving actions that bring individual and communal unity, or hateful ones that alienate us from our trust of self, neighbor and God. Do our choices ferment a society that values community, seeking the welfare of the least, rather than a predatory one that victimizes the elderly and exploits the many for the profit of the few? Do our governments pursue policies that promote the general good, or do they espouse those that have a narrow benefit? Can the mission of a corporation simply be the pursuit of profits without regard for the interests of their employees or society?

Similarly, the world community impacts our individual health as we are either nurtured or assailed by the flow of human events. A society dominated by materialistic values as well as drugs and violence, creates a poisonous atmosphere for the pursuit of health. An alienated community characterized by lawlessness, injustice, and disharmony births violent communal members. The health of the individual and that of the community are mutually dependent. A stable community with life-affirming values and an infrastructure for caring, births the development of healthy members. The health of a community may be judged by its unity and the pursuit of humanistic and transcendent values such as mercy, peace, justice and service.

As care providers we are obligated to choose health with all of its ramifications. Our quest for health of body, mind and soul will have consequences, not only for ourselves, but also for our loved ones and our community, because the healing of humanity's heart begins with the healing of our own.

Today, let us begin the journey. Let us seek to "harden not our hearts" to the cry of those who suffer and pursue our mission of mercy. Let us obey the faint, whispering echoes rambling in the cavernous recesses of the wounded as well as in our own broken hearts—"Love one another—May they be one."

REFERENCES

Cannon, N.J. (1987). The broken healer. *Humane Medicine*, 3(2), 121–23.

——. (1992). How tender our wounds: A meditation on competence in caring. *Humane Medicine*, 8(7), 231–37.

Clarke, J. (1977). *St. Therese of Lisieux: Her last conversations.* Washington, D.C.: Institute of Carmelite Studies.

Dashiff C., Greiner, D.S., and Cannon, N.J. (1990). Physician and nurse collaboration in a medical indigent clinic. *Family Systems Medicine,* 8, 57–70.

Goodloe, N.R., and Arreola, P. M. (1992). Spiritual health: Out of the closet. *Journal of Health Education,* 23(4), 221–26.

Greiner, D. S. and Cannon, H. J. (1991). I sent myself a card today. In D. Gaut and M. Leininger (Eds.). *Caring: The compassionate healer* (pp. 115–21). New York: National League for Nursing Press.

Kohn, A. (1991). Caring kids: The role of the school. *Phi Delta Kappan,* 72(7), 496–506.

Linn, D. and Linn, M. (1972). *Healing life's hurts.* New York: Paulist Press.

MacNutt, F. (1977). *The power to heal.* Notre Dame, Indiana: Ave Maria Press.

Maher, M. F. and Hunt, T. K. (1993). Spirituality reconsidered. *Counseling and Values,* 38, 21–28.

Merton, T. (1971). *Contemplative prayer.* New York: Doubleday and Co.

Nouwen, H. J. M. (1979). *The wounded healer.* New York: Doubleday and Co.

Roach, M. S. (1992). *The human act of caring: A blueprint for the health professions* (Rev. ed.). Ottawa: Canadian Hospital Assoc.

Starck, P. L., and McGovern, J. P. (Eds.). (1992). *The hidden dimension of illness: Human suffering.* New York: National League for Nursing Press.

Thayer-Bacon, B.J. (1993). Caring and its relationship to critical thinking. *Educational Theory,* 43(3), 233–240.

van Breeman, P.G. (1974). *As bread that is broken.* Denville, N.J.: Dimension Books.

Ward, B. (1975). *The sayings of the desert fathers.* Oxford: A. R. Mowbray and Co.

Names and identifying characteristics of the patients referred to in this paper have been changed to protect their privacy.

Healing the Fractured Self

Mary-Therese B. Dombeck

Introduction

> A student asks his teacher, "I have a question about
> Deuteronomy 6:6 which says: 'and these words which I com-
> mand you this day, shall be upon your heart.' Why is it said
> this way? Why are we not told to place them in our heart?"
> The teacher responds, "It is not within the power of human
> beings to place the divine teaching directly in their hearts.
> All we can do is place them on the surface of the heart so
> that when the heart breaks they drop in."
>
> Paraphrased from Buber, *Tales of the Hasidim*

Spiritual[1] awareness[2] involves being attentive to one's spirit and
to what is of ultimate concern in one's life. Although all human
persons are defined by their human spirit, not all human persons
are attentive to this dimension of themselves. Dreams provide
the opportunity for spiritual awareness, and some dreams, by the
quality and intensity of their imagery, help us to give these ultimate issues the depth and intensity they deserve.

In this paper the dream experience of a twenty-nine-year-
old woman is presented as an example conducive to spiritual
reflection. The dream is regarded as a cultural story of construction and fracturing of self in western industrial societies.
Pathways to healing are also addressed.

Before introducing the dream I refer briefly to the story of
the student and the teacher in the introductory paragraph. The
story is told in the context of the Jewish pietistic movement of
Hasidism. The teacher is the pious rabbi whose wisdom is typically relational and dialogical. The student learns by asking the
rabbi questions about the relationships between persons, and

between God and each person. In that context the student and the teacher both assume the heart to be the unifying center of the physical and psychic life of each person, the seat of the emotions, intellect, courage, volition, morality and conscience. The heart is also the point of contact with the Torah, the divine instruction and guidance. Therefore, the heart in that context signifies one's personhood (Buttrick, 1962). The lesson is that the heart is often made hospitable to divine guidance by being broken. The meaning of "broken" here is multidimensional. On the one hand, it conveys all the nuances of "brokenhearted," namely fractured, grieved, suffering, humbled, softened. However, it also has the connotation of "opening," of making an opening through to a wider space, to a freer space, as in escaping or breaking through the womb to be born.

The twentieth-century dreamer whose dream is presented in this paper does not use the heart as a symbol in her dream. In our context the heart is often understood to mean literally the cardiac muscle and alternately and metaphorically, the seat of emotion, caring, compassion, affection and love. However, we typically separate the literal and metaphorical meanings of heart. In our world our organs (hearts, lungs, kidneys) can be unilaterally removed and transplanted. Helman (1991) in contemplating the technical reality of the first heart transplant he witnessed, said:

> Now for the first time one of the most important metaphors for personhood had been cut out, handled and cleaned, and then placed inside the body of another individual. In a few historic moments, the borders of one human body had been breached by the symbolic core of another. (P.2)

In our context it is hard to think of the heart as an organizing principle. It is not surprising that the dream of the twenty-nine-year-old woman was not about a heart but about a "face" and a "mirror image," although in her dream there was also brokenness and splintering.

The Dream of Fractured Face

I am looking in the mirror; actually I'm looking for wrinkles before applying my make-up. I think I detect one, but no, this is a crack in the mirror exactly where the wrinkle must be on my face. This is surprising. I don't remember the mirror being cracked. As I get closer to the mirror, I see that the crack is longer than I thought. As I look closely I notice there are many cracks in the mirror. My surprise changes to concern because the squiggly cracks are now all over my mirror face. Two long cracks in the mirror—one vertical and one horizontal have actually divided my face into four quarters. Now the mirror is a quartered, splintered mess.

I raise my hand to feel my face in order to be reassured. But it feels like splintered glass. I am horrified. I feel glass splinters in my fingers. They are bleeding, and the drops of blood from my fingers are appearing as red spots on the mirror face. I awaken in terror.

She was agitated and animated as she told me the dream. She said it was so realistic that she thought she was awake even as she was dreaming. As I listened, I wondered what it might be like to have such a dream, or to consider that such a dream might be my personal story. She might be horrified by the possibility that the dream is telling her story, and she might be trying to distance herself from the experience. She is coming to me for an interpretation which could be introduced between her dream and her experience of it. In fact, I find myself trying to do the same thing. My own interpretations of the dream begin introducing themselves amidst my experience of the dream, the woman and myself. As westerners in a society that values rationality and causality, we start to make psychological interpretations and ascribe causes to dreams from a distance like this:

Maybe this woman is just realizing that she was more deeply hurt than she knew; maybe she has been battered, abused, raped, and her personality has splintered, and this is one of the rare times when she has caught a glimpse of the many pieces; maybe she is finding a crack in her narcissism; maybe she should stop applying make-up; maybe she can no longer cover up her chemical dependency; maybe she is ill; she has a physical condition which is cracking her psychic life and her social relations. Maybe it's not that at all; maybe she is starting therapy and is beginning to feel some pain; she is afraid it will be intolerable. She is afraid to "lose face"; to lose her previous self. The interpretations go on and on, and we get further and further away from our own experience of a dream whether it's our own dream or someone else's.

However, this dream does not allow the dreamer or the hearer to distance from it. It moves us to contemplate the mysterious changes that occur in the two symbols in the dream, namely the "face" and the "mirror." The dreamer communicated her horror to me. But even if she had not done so herself, even if I had encountered her dream apart from her, on a printed page, as you are encountering it now, it would have inspired awe in me. The dream draws me and repels me at the same time. Because I have seen brokenness and splintering in others and in myself, it tells me a story that on the one hand, I recognize, and on the other hand, seems to defy understanding. It delivers an urgent surrealist message about the "face" and the "self." Maybe the "self" is made of glass and not of flesh; maybe it is more shattered and less whole than I had anticipated, and maybe the mirror-image reflection is more accurately a reflection of the self than I had anticipated. When a dream speaks with such urgency and intensity about ultimate human issues as wholeness, brokenness, suffering and reflection, it represents a cultural or universal image as well as a personal one. Even though the twenty-nine-year-old woman and I worked on her particular learnings from the dream, those will not be the focus of this paper. In this paper the dream will be explored as a cultural image or modern myth.

The Dream as Cultural Image or Modern Myth

Dreams are symbolic stories we tell ourselves and others by making pictures out of our words. Dreams tell personal stories, and because a person is always situated in a social and linguistic context, dreams, like myths, also tell cultural stories. Sometimes the dream of a single human being can tell the story of a historical period. So this twenty-nine-year-old woman can be Anywoman or Anyman in the late twentieth century.

In this dream the face in front of the mirror is literally and symbolically face to face with itself. The mirror reflects the face in front of it as the woman reflects on herself. Spiritual awareness begins when one notices and is willing to engage new information about oneself and about one's world. Dreams provide a means to spiritual awareness because they place personal images in social, cultural, and mythical contexts, and make them available to our experience.

Social, Cultural and Mythical Contexts

The words "mirror" and "face" are recognizable symbols, not only to the dreamer but also to the hearers and readers of this dream. In our context faces and mirrors are ubiquitous. They are to be found in the inside and outside of buildings, on billboards, storefronts, elevators, restrooms, homes, private and public rooms. Persons are faced with images of themselves and others wherever they go, whether they want to see them or not. There are reminders everywhere of how the "beautiful people" look, and reminders about how one ought to appear to others. So persons absent-mindedly or anxiously look at other faces and at themselves in mirrors. This has been called the Age of Narcissism (Lasch, 1978, 1984). It is not surprising that a dream of a "mirror" and a "face" that is splintered, should so urgently grab the attention of the dreamer, the hearer and the reader.

The word "mirror" comes from the Latin word *mirrare* meaning "to wonder at." The mirror has an interesting history. It is a material artifact that humans have manufactured in different eras and in different civilizations. Early mirrors such as those used by the Greeks and Romans consisted of disks of polished metal. When the Biblical Paul wrote in his well-known letter to the Corinthians (probably written in the first midcentury A.D.), "Now I see through a glass darkly," or paraphrased "Now, I see in a mirror indistinctly," it was because a mirror at that time, even a very good mirror, projected an indistinct image at best. The indistinctness was increased by the fact that it was not easy to make a mirror plane or flat enough to project an accurate image. Surfaces were often slightly curved. In fact it was common to use convex or concave mirrors to create special kinds of images. A convex mirror enlarges the image. A concave mirror makes things look farther away, and condenses a large area like a telescope, as do rearview mirrors in cars.

Symbolically, then, because of its capacity to change the appearance of the size of things, a mirror became associated with imagination, consciousness and divination. Now in the twentieth century, a mirror image reflects what we call "the real world" with such verisimilitude that it has become the symbol for clarity on the one hand, and on the other hand, one is surprised when realizing that the mirror image has little depth[3]. The point of remembering the history of mirrors is that mirrors have depicted the cultural images of the self in different ages of our history: the self of Narcissus, the beautiful self, the ugly self, the inflated ego, the diviner, the magician who "does it with mirrors," and the two-way mirror in psychotherapeutic practice. The etymology of the word "face" is from the Latin facies, signifying appearance, aspect or form. Literally, when we talk about "face," we mean the front of the head. A person's face is what he/she looks like to the rest of the world. We also talk about the "face" of a card, document or book, the front part of a building. "Face" also has a connotation of an outward covering whether the outward covering is cursory or superficial or dignified. The general sense of the word "face" is one of giving form or shape to the self. It connotes an action of construction.

The Constructed Self

How is the self constructed in our society, that is, given face and shaped? A child born in the twentieth century in a complex industrial society is expected to have a self, or be a self. As the child grows and develops, it is preferred and made known by parents and teachers that the sense of self be robust (not weak); unitary (not multiple); well-bounded (not diffuse); autonomous (not dependent). This is felt by all, especially those who are functional and successful in the society. There are many more adjectives used to describe the self, and many nuances to the word self are created by hyphenating the word self in conjunction with another word. The self is ubiquitous in popular (Eliot, 1909) and scholarly literature (Hewitt, 1989; Whittaker, 1992; Krieger,

1991). Words like self-esteem, self-image, self-actualization, self-concept, are used in textbooks as well as on afternoon talk shows on television, on the evening news and on psychological pop quizzes in the newspaper and in cartoons. There is now a *Self* magazine. It contains a collection of articles with advice about the body and the psyche. So our social environment, far from being indifferent to the construction of self, is quite hospitable to it, and even openly mandates it.

In the scholarly communities the self is also examined, constructed, debated or refuted. I will mention only very briefly and specifically a few theories on the formation of the self. I chose these particular ones because they contain, along with the metaphor of self, the image of the mirror and of reflection. The sociologist Cooley (1902) actually uses the term "looking glass self," to describe the influence of social relations on the self. Mead (1934) conceptualizes a symbolic interaction between how others see me and how I see myself. Sullivan (1953) makes this interaction look like a mirror when he talks about a baby's capacity to recognize itself only through the face of the mothering one. Kohut postulates that a cohesive self is possible only in the presence of the empathic mirroring by the self object (Kohut and Wolf, 1978). For Kohut the self is cohesive, bounded and autonomous. He calls it "an independent centre of initiative" (p. 414). Lacan (1977) also uses the mirror image but, in contrast to Kohut, says that the child actually feels fragmented, and in order to compensate for this, constructs its image of wholeness by identifying itself with the image of another's wholeness. For Lacan, the purpose of therapy is to undermine the false sense of a unified self by encouraging new contradictory "split" meanings to emerge, and to reveal that behind the apparent unity of meanings lies a diversity of meanings.

Controversies about the self abound in scholarly literature. Whether the self is an agentic subject or a passive object (Deci and Ryan, 1990), whether the perceived cohesion of the self is an illusion or a reality (Ewing, 1990; DeMunck, 1992), whether the male and female selves have similar or different developmental courses (Miller-McLemore, 1991), and whether the self is essential or contingent (Rorty, 1989). Whatever the arguments, it is clear that the self is a very important topic. There may not be a single model or understanding of exactly what the self should be in our contemporary western experience; there seems to be not only a popular encouragement for its creation, but also a scholarly mandate and prescription for thoughts and writings about how it is constructed.

The Fracture of Self

Let us reflect on personal experiences of self. Who am I? Who am I when I am alone? Who am I when I am with you? Who am I when I am with an intimate friend? with my superior? with my beloved? with my nurse? with my physician? Who am I when I feel known? when I feel only partially known? Are these selves the same? Which one of these selves is the strongest, the best known to me? how was it nurtured so that it would thrive? and most importantly, at the expense of what other parts of me? Some of these selves are recognized and rewarded, so they grow, and we like showing them to best advantage. For example, the responsible, competitive parts of a self may have been rewarded at the expense of the childlike, hospitable parts of oneself. Usually there are stereotypes about oneself that were assigned experientially in one's past development that have become permanent parts of one's identity: the responsible one, the irresponsible one, the black sheep, the one with the temper, the bright one, the tough one, the looser.

There are many parts to the self, nurtured or neglected by the social or the inner environment. There are parts of the self unknown or incompatible with other parts of the self, that are forgotten or lost when old environments are no longer there. An eighty-five-year-old woman, weeping for the loss of her friend, blurted out that this was the last person who knew her when she was young. Without someone remembering her self with her, she felt a loss not only of her friend, but of her own self. She is starting to feel not only alone, but also isolated.

Gender issues are extremely important in contributing to the fracturing of the self *and* to its healing. In the dream it is a woman who looks anxiously for wrinkles in a society where aging women are devalued. Gender issues cannot be ignored in our personal lives and our social lives. All of us are either male or female, so we all know something about the construction of gender in ourselves. We know the experience of our anatomy and physiology as it is situated in tacitly learned or openly accepted meanings of our social life. How does it feel to be me—a woman? What does it mean to me, to be a woman at my job? How did I feel as a man when I got my first "good job"? and when I lost it? How am I with men friends? with women friends? How is my role at my job construed for me as man or as woman? How does my gender contribute to, or block my chances for the future. These are questions we need to ask ourselves because the polarization of the male and female principles in our social structures and in our individual selves is one of the most important aspects of the construction and the fracturing of selves.[4]

Both women and men suffer from this polarization of the feminine and masculine principles in the construction of self but in different ways (Miller-McLemore, 1991). A man who notices his face in the mirror and feels the fracture might want to call into question the inflexible necessity of always having to be a hero or a villain, strong, bounded, cohesive and autonomous. A woman who notices her face in the mirror might want to question why the only categories for selfhood usually allowed to a woman are ones which contrast with the masculine hero, strong, bounded, cohesive and autonomous. Both men and women become marginalized in our society when they are least like the mandated construction of self.

In complex industrial societies our selves have a tendency to be cut up in compartmentalized contexts. In any one of these contexts we seem to be known only in part, and we are only required to show ourselves in part. Douglas, (1970), talks eloquently about the breadth and numbers of social relations which are possible, and she raises questions about their depth. She says:

> How many social relationships can anyone have at any one time? Fifty? A hundred? Probably no more within the meaning of the word. The milkman who delivers milk and is paid, the lawyer who is consulted, the office colleagues who are rarely seen outside the office, the old friends and cousins

whose relationship has dwindled to an exchange of cards, the personal element is extremely attenuated in those relationships. Suppose we take fifty friends and relations arbitrarily as representing the capacity of the average individual to enter and sustain personal relations—then we can ask concerning those fifty how close-knit and regular is the web of reciprocity? (p. 62)

Gabel (1988) gives a description in a moving account of a bank teller. While at work the bank teller, especially the one who is new at his role, in order to fit in the bank, somehow feels himself "outside" of himself and "inside" the role of bank teller. The bank teller has to learn to act "as if" he were a bank teller for a few hours every day. The new bank teller will continue to indoctrinate herself on how to be a successful bank teller by taking her cues from others in her environment. These others are primarily known to her as other bank tellers, supervisors and customers. Gabel continues eloquently, "Ontological passivity is, therefore, a collective experience that simultaneously divides a group of people by an infinite distance and unites them in the false communion of being other than themselves together" (p. 44). Our work places, even the good ones, provide fragmenting experiences because we seldom can *show* and *be* large portions of ourselves while at work. Suppose the bank teller was in love, depressed or afraid. Who could she tell? Are the roles of lover or depressed person acceptable? Suppose she is gay? A large portion of herself would have to remain secret unless she is willing to put herself at risk, and put that part of herself under a symbolic microscope. As a consequence other parts of herself, namely the ordinary inconspicuous self that meets casually and talks naturally to others, might be ignored as she is scrutinized "out of the closet" by others who will, from now on, only pay attention to the one stereotyped part.

The bank is usually thought of as a good place to work. People who work in factories wished they worked in banks. In factories the mechanization and potential for fragmentation is more blatant and less subtle. Not only is the factory worker relating to others *primarily,* or *exclusively* as a coworker or supervisor, but also there is a practical relationship with machines. If, at times, it occurs to her that the machine is an extension of her hands, at other times, it must occur to her that she is an extension of the machine. This mechanical self-definition is corroborated by the values in the workplace. When the economic *bottom line* is threatened, it is the person, not the machine, that loses the job. So, paradoxically, in a culture known for its narcissism, and preoccupied with individual identity, it is difficult to experience a sense of self.

So far, I have not considered persons who have had a particularly traumatic self construction or childhood. What I have described are just issues that arise naturally from living in complex industrial societies. When persons sustain very traumatic experiences, like abuse and severe illness, these are added to the beleaguered and tenuous sense of self. Whatever the degree of trauma, the pathways to healing involve a symbolic *awakening,* a receptivity or *hospitality* to new learnings, and a *commitment* to intentionally tend to the *practical activities of healing.*

PATHWAYS TO HEALING

Awakening

The construction of the self is often the occasion and the reason for its fracturing. It is hard, and even impossible to live up to, or understand mandates and prescriptions for a strong, unified, autonomous, bounded and whole image of the self. Most persons recognize that they do not conform to the accepted image.

The dream of the fractured face begins by the dreamer "looking for" wrinkles, and "noticing" many cracks. The dream gives her information that she would rather not remember, and it does so by introducing the dream into her waking life. She could have ignored the dream and distanced herself from it by forgetting what she saw or by dismissing it as "just a dream." She did not do these things. Instead, she took the dream seriously. She honored the dream by *taking notice of it,* and by inviting a witness to "see" it with her. It is much easier to deceive oneself privately than in the presence of another.

Awakening is a metaphor for "becoming conscious": to become aware of things that were previously unconscious; not only about oneself but also about one's context. Awakening is a symbol for becoming alert to patterns, consistencies and inconsistencies in the symbolic and social structures that define one's situation. Not only self-understanding but also social transformations begin by dreaming, taking notice, awakening and telling witnesses. The civil rights movement, the feminist movement and other human rights movements were inspired by women and men who had the courage to let their "dreams"⁵ and other new awarenesses engage their waking life. These awakened persons also saw the need and had the courage to invite others to *see* and *hear* the "dream" with them. Personal and social transformations are usually preceded by consciousness-raising activities, where awakenings are shared. Often, what is brought to awareness is the reality of what is divided, fragmented and negative in one's life.⁶

Choosing not to notice personal and social realities is a barrier to symbolic awakening and spiritual awareness. In the language of the dream this would be analogous to distancing oneself from the mirror so that one's image is reduced in size and clarity, giving the illusion of a fictitious wholeness. This perpetuates pseudo-innocence and self-deception. Another barrier to spiritual awareness is choosing to circumscribe one's conscious awareness only to selected, familiar and acceptable portions of oneself, such as a particular social role. In the symbolic language of the dream this would be analogous to confining one's awareness to one or two small unfractured pieces of oneself, and of one's world. Thus large portions of oneself remain unknown and alien. Life becomes reduced and impoverished. The initial simplicity of this response to the knowledge that the self is fractured is gradually complicated by a need to defend against and suppress whatever is perceived as unfamiliar, alien, or new. This was not the response of the twenty-nine-year-old woman.

Hospitality

The twenty-nine-year-old woman who had the dream of the fractured face was receptive to her dream. She did not dismiss it.

She was open to exploring it. Receptivity enhances spiritual awareness by inviting into one's consciousness whatever might be of ultimate concern in life. It is a quality of hospitality.[7] Nouwen (1979) describes hospitality as "the virtue which allows us to break through the narrowness of our own fears and to open our house to the stranger, with the intuition that salvation comes to us in the form of a tired traveler." When attention is given to the learnings of the dream, it is not a distanced objective attentiveness, but an embodied one. It is an invitation to the subjective dream experience and message. The dream of the fractured face is an invitation to consider the fracturing as part of the healing.

The attitude and practice of hospitality toward one's dream can open one to the practice of hospitality to new ideas, beliefs and to persons. There is a possibility of new tolerance, born out of the reality that one is wounded and broken, to empathize with others who are wounded and broken. Hospitality makes one willing to converse and negotiate with what was previously unknown, intolerable or unwanted. One is more open to new possibilities and complexities. Nouwen (1979) and Downing (1991) both emphasize that only the wounded healer can heal. Downing (1991) traces the image of the wounded healer in myths and rituals of traditional preindustrial societies, and Nouwen (1979) talks of the helper and minister as wounded healer in contemporary society. It is an understanding that in postindustrial complex societies the path to healing begins by recognizing human contingency and insufficiency, especially one's own. Self-help groups and associations like twelve step programs are also based on the same understanding. These groups make it possible for persons to share with each other the awareness of brokenness, and the openness and commitment to healing.

Commitment to Healing

Just as hospitality involves tending to the guest, so receptivity to one's dream usually results in practical action. It is important that awarenesses from a dream is engaged in one's waking life. Often it is the dream itself that gives a clue to such action.

In the dream, after observing that the mirror is cracked, the woman realizes that:

> Two long cracks—one vertical and one horizontal have actually divided my face into four quarters.

Amid the chaotic random fracturing of the mirror face there is a hint of order as the vertical line and the horizontal line intersect. It is after this that the woman touches her face. Thus the disembodied image of her mirror face becomes connected to her real, wounded face. If the vertical line symbolizes spiritual awareness and transcendence, it is important that these understandings be connected to the horizontal contextual situation including all the relationships that it represents. Moore (1992) considers that a life steeped only in transcendence is in danger of becoming narrowly fundamentalist. Conversely a life mired and bogged down without transcendence becomes dispirited and hopeless.

The third pathway to healing involves a commitment to intentionally pursue practical actions in the interest of healing. These experiences and actions are described by James as a way of salvation and a religious experience (1961/1901). He described the experience using dramatic metaphors of fragmentation and of being rescued from drowning. He said that persons sometimes experience different parts to themselves and become conscious that the "higher part is coterminous and continuous with a MORE of the same quality, which is operative in the universe outside of him, and which he can keep in touch with, and in a fashion, get on board of and save himself when all his lower being has gone to pieces in the wreck" (p. 393-394).

Concluding Remarks

In this paper the dream of a twenty-nine-year-old woman was presented as an example conducive to spiritual reflection. The dream was regarded as a cultural story of the construction and fracturing of self. The dream was not interpreted. It was told, heard and experienced.

I return briefly to the image of the broken heart introduced in the story of the student and the teacher on the first page. In that context the student and teacher both assume that the heart is the unifying center of the physical and psychic life of each person.[8] The dream of the twenty-nine-year old woman presents us, from a postindustrialist point of view, with the image of a fractured, splintered self. One could ask where the seat of the emotions, intellect, courage, volition, morality and conscience is for such a person! Is this a time and place of blatantly amoral, anti-intellectual fragmented selves? It would seem so at times. However, the symbolism in the dream also points to the possibility that the "heart" is in the fractured pieces and in the cracks. In the dream all the cracks are not random. The order and healing appear in connections. The connections are between the vertical and horizontal dimensions of life, between dream life and waking life and between dream teller and dream hearer, between individual and communal or social understanding.

Reflection on dreams can be a pathway to healing. It involves a commitment to intentional and sustained involvement in the following activities: remembering the dream and retelling it in the presence of others (if it is one's own), writing it down, listening to it, studying the symbols, connecting them to one's personal and social life, being hospitable to the dream by taking the learnings inside, and trying to enact them practically in one's life and in one's world.

For the caregiver, dreams can be a means to healing oneself and, moreover, they can provide an opportunity to listen to whatever fragments of a person's life is revealed in the telling. For it is in being the *listened to* that selves are retold and reconnected.

REFERENCES

Ayto, J. (1990). *Dictionary of Word Origins.* New York: Arcade Publishing, Little Brown.

Buttrick, G.A., (Ed.) (1962). *The Interpreter's Dictionary of the Bible,* (Vol. 1). New York: Abington Press.

Cooley, C.H. (1902). *Human Nature and the Social Order.* New York: Scribner's.

Deci, E.L. and Ryan, R. M. (1990). A motivational approach to the self: Integration of personality. *Nebraska Symposium on Motivation,* 240–86.

DeMunck, V. (1992). The fallacy of the misplaced self: Gender relations and construction of multiple selves among Sri Lankan Muslims, *Ethos: J. of the Society for Psychological Anthropology,* 20(2), 167–90.

Dombeck, M. T. (1989). The contexts of caring: Conscience and consciousness in caring: *The Compassionate Healer,* (Eds. Gaut and Leininger), 19–36.

Douglas, M. (1970). Natural Symbols—Explorations in Cosmology. New York: Pantheon Books.

Downing, C. (ed.) (1991). *Mirrors of the Self: Archetypal Images That Shape Your Life.* Los Angeles: J. P. Tarcher, Inc.

Eliot, C. W. (ed.) (1937, 1909). *Folklore and Fable: Aesop, Grimm, Anderson.* New York: P. F. Collier and Son.

Ewing, K. (1990). The illusion of wholeness: Culture, self and the experience of inconsistency, *Ethos: J. of the Society for Psychological Anthropology,* 18(3), 251–78.

Gabel, P. (1988). The Bank Teller. *Tikkun,* 2(1), 44–49.

Helman, C. (1991). *The Body of Frankenstein's Monster: Essays in Myth and Medicine.* New York: W. W. Norton Co.

Hewitt, J. P. (1989). *Dilemmas of the American Self.* Philadelphia: Temple University Press.

James, W. (1961/1902). *The Varieties of Religious Experience: A Study in Human Nature.* New York: Collier Books, Macmillan.

Krieger, S. (1991). *Social Science and the Self. Personal Essays on an Art Form.* New Brunswick: Rutgers University Press.

Lacan, J. (1977). *Ecrits: A Selection.* New York: Norton.

Lasch, C. (1978). *The Culture of Narcissism: American in an Age of Diminishing Expectation.* New York: Norton.

——. (1984). *The Minimal Self: Psychic Survival in Troubled Times.* New York: W. Norton and Co.

LeGuin, U. K. (1969). *The Left Hand of Darkness.* New York: Walker.

——. (1979). *The Language of the Night.* New York: Berkeley Books.

Mead, G.H. (1934). *Mind, Self and Society.* Chicago: The University of Chicago Press.

Miller-McLemore, B.J. (1991). Women who work and love: Caught between cultures. In *Women in Travail & Transition.* (eds. Glaz and Moessner).

Moore, T. (1992). *Care of the Soul.* New York: HarperCollins.

Nouwen, H. J. M. (1979). *The Wounded Healer,* New York: Image Books, Doubleday.

Rorty, R. (1989). The contingency of self in *Contingency, Irony and Solidarity.* New York: Cambridge, Cambridge University Press.

Sullivan, H. S. (1953). *The Interpersonal Theory of Psychiatry*. New York: W. W. Norton.

Whittaker, E. (1992). The birth of the anthropological self. *Ethos: J. of the Society of Psychological Anthropology*, 20(2), 191–219.

NOTES

1. The word *spirit* derives from the Latin word **spiritus**, the meaning of which encompasses the concepts of breath, air and wind. Moreover, because of its connection to the word **anima**, the word "spirit" is often related etymologically to "soul" or "self." "Spirit" in Hebrew is **ruah** or air wind. "Spirit" literally refers to what gives life to, or animates, a **nefesh** or "self" (Ayto,1990).

2. The word "awareness" derives from the Germanic word **ware** which connotes watching, attending to, taking care, and even being on one's guard.

3. Our literature, science fiction, art forms and expressive arts have imagined, created, and invented stories of a whole other world paralleling to the one in the mirror. In *Alice in the Looking Glass, Snow White, Star Trek, Tales of Hoffman* and *Phantom of the Opera,* the mirrors are used as symbols of entering a different world. Visual artists have told stories of persons using mirrors: convex, concave, plane and glass mirrors.

4. Ursula LeGuin wrote a story about a world where biological gender differences did not define people for all their lives but only during reproductive cycles (1969). In one of her nonfiction essays she describes myths and sub-myths:

> Superman was a sub-myth. "Other science-fictional sub-myths are the blond heroes of sword and sorcery, with their usual weapons..., benevolent dictators; brave starship captains, evil aliens, good aliens and the ever pointy-breasted brainless young woman who was even rescued, lectured to, patronized, or raped by one of the aforementioned heroes." (1979, p. 67)

She continued to say that our central problem is "exploitation of the woman, of the weak, of the earth: and that "our curse is alienation, the separation of yang and yin" (p. 159).

5. The word "dream" is used here in its double meaning of "a series of images, thoughts, and emotions occurring during sleep" and

"a strongly desired goal or purpose." I believe that the latter meaning is often contained in the former.

6. William James, the pragmatist psychologist, described the acknowledgment of the experience of a divided self as the first step to a process of personal unification (1961/1902): "to be conscious of a negation is already virtually to be beyond it. The mere asking of a question or expression or a dissatisfaction proves that the answer or the satisfaction is already imminent" (1961/1902, p. 351).

7. The word "hospitality" is connected to the words "hospital" or "hospice" or "hostel," which describe an institution for the care of the needy, aged, infirm, young or dying (Ayto, 1990).

8. Even William James (1961/1902), as late as 1902, described the saintly person as one whose heart has become "broken" or "softened": "The stone wall inside of him has fallen, the hardness in his heart has broken down" (p. 217).

Caring, Spirituality and Suffering

Katie Eriksson

Caring from the heart draws one into the reality of human suffering. As a human experience, suffering can be described; as a mystery, suffering eludes human comprehension. These reflections focus on what it means to be a human person, and highlights the capacity each person has for compassion and unconditional love.

Caring, Spirituality and Suffering

> "...what is man that thou art mindful of him? and the son of man, that thou visitest him? For thou hast made him a little lower than the angels, and hast crowned him with glory and honour...." (Psalms 8:4-5)

The human being as an inviolable divine entity, suffering as part of all human life, and caring as a manifestation of the human person's ability to feel compassion and unconditional love, belong together. All types of caring originate from two sources—motherliness or spontaneous love which we can regard as natural care; and compassion and mercy on which professional care is based. To have the courage to see your neighbor's suffering and to assume responsibility to alleviate it without just walking by, are the responses in which all care originates. Professional care has been described in the story of the Good Samaritan, told for the first time in the story of mercy in the valley of the Nile (cf. Vonhoff, 1962).

The idea of motherliness implies two fundamental

processes in all human relationships—to nourish and to purify. Every person needs nourishment and purification of body, soul and spirit (cf. Eriksson, 1987). Originally, the act of caring was a natural human response in all cultures. Cultural patterns and the ways of realizing care varied, but the purpose was the same— to help the human person live a worthy life. Gradually, as native cultures took on practices of other developed civilizations, their spiritual beliefs were neglected (cf. Berdjajev, 1990).

Within modern western culture, emerging as it did within a mechanistic paradigm, the core values of mercy, compassion and love receded into the background. This unfortunate fact has been reflected in nursing practice being reduced to a job in the service of a health system where a human person's value is determined by money and the capacity to produce. The patient, no longer a suffering human being, is a customer who buys the services offered by the system. We now experience a turning point where once again we have to articulate and take a stand on the foundations of nursing and its basic human values. Within nursing this raises the issue of identity and presents a challenge for caring science as a whole.

What is identified as caring does not always contribute to the alleviation of the patient's suffering. Such "non care" actually causes suffering. In studies about suffering carried out in Finland (Eriksson, 1992; Lindholm and Eriksson, 1993), we have found that specific approaches to care often cause patient suffering. We have called this "suffering caused by caring." The main reasons for such suffering are violation of human dignity, condemnation, abuse of power and lack of care itself. Even Florence Nightingale (1869) describes this in her book, *Notes on Nursing*.

> In watching disease, both in private houses and in public hospitals, the thing which strikes the experienced observer most forcibly is this: that the symptoms or the sufferings generally considered to be inevitable and incident to the disease are very often not symptoms of the disease at all, but of something quite different—of the want of fresh air, or of light, or of warmth, or of quiet, or of cleanliness, or of punctuality and care in the administration of diet, of each or of all of these....The reparative process which nature has instituted and which we call disease has been hindered by some

want of knowledge or attention, in one or in all of these things, and pain, suffering, or interruption of the whole process sets in.... If a patient is cold, if a patient is feverish, if a patient is faint, if he is sick after taking food, if he has a bed-sore, it is generally the fault not of the disease, but of the nursing. (Pp. 5-6)

Professional care which aims at nursing the whole human person must repudiate all forms of care which cause suffering, because such care cannot be regarded as care.

The Whole Human Being

Being healthy means being whole, experiencing oneself as a whole person. The experience of wholeness implies in its deepest sense an experience of "holiness," reverence for one's own life, for oneself as a human being and as someone unique. The concept of health is derived from the Old Swedish word *hel* (holy), and "salvation." The human being's experience of being "holy" presupposes that he is in contact with his innermost core, his spirituality and religiousness.

The human being, created by God in His own image, is an entity of body, soul and spirit. The human being is basically religious but not everyone has accepted this dimension (cf. Barbosa da Silva and Eriksson, 1991). A human being can experience and express the spiritual phenomena as existential, religious and/or Christian.

The experience of holiness is a religious experience, something of a fundamental experience for a human being. This experience is an important source of strength, and in order to be a whole person, the human person must again and again be able to return to the original state of wholeness. Eriksson (1959) calls this process rebirth; Eliade (1968) calls it new creation; Tillich (1952) views it as the foundation for experience, and it implies the courage to exist. This basic experience implies the source of faith and hope which, as well as love, are basic sources of strength throughout life.

Caring of the whole human being presupposes that we understand and accept the patient's spiritual experiences irrespective of his way of expressing them. A professional nurse should be able to recognize and, to a certain extent, meet the patient's spiritual needs and demands irrespective of her own personal attitude to spirituality and religion.

Human Dignity

A person whose dignity is violated, suffers. Human dignity is connected to the most fundamental value of caring, that is, to unprejudiciously confirm the patient's absolute dignity as a human being. Absolute human dignity is grounded in one's humanity. In this respect, all human persons are equal and inviolable. Caring which concerns the whole person starts with the confirmation of human dignity and the incalculable worth of the human person. As noted above, human dignity is often violated in certain patterns of practice, patterns of care which cannot be called caring in its authentic sense.

Dignity is an essential attribute of the human person and, in the biblical sense, derived from one's creation in the image of God. A person experiences dignity when he or she is able to express the human capacity to be available to serve and to be there for another. When a person is deprived of the ability to care and the responsibility to act accordingly, human dignity is violated. Human dignity also includes freedom to make one's own choices in life, as well as the right to protect oneself from infringement (cf. Lindborg, 1974, 1991).

The idea of absolute human dignity has its origin in Christian humanism. Even though secular humanism emphasizes the value and freedom of the human being, it must still be regarded as insufficient if it should serve as a starting point for ethically advanced caring. The absolute ethical is to be found in our acceptance of absolute human dignity and of our inviolability in all respects. Caring which is truly ethical repudiates any form of condemnation, abuse of power, punishment, and different forms of service in which caring has failed to occur.

The issues of human responsibility and dignity have not always been self-evident or unambiguous. Skinner (1973) tried to overthrow the idea of personal responsibility. His position was that most difficulties caused by human beings could be overcome by a kind of behavioral technology, which meant that a human being could be programmed to behave correctly. It is the idea of the autonomous human being, his freedom and supposed dignity which prevents a person from correct behavior. According to Skinner, the notion of a person who is free and conscious of his responsibilities should be abolished; by that he says that we shall abolish the idea of human dignity (cf. Stott, 1986). The Skinnerian idea has permeated modern care and, consequently, the human being has been deprived in many respects of responsibility and dignity.

When studying the history of nursing, one becomes aware of how nurses have always had to struggle in order to maintain the dignity of the human being and to uphold his absolute value. In the struggle, nurses have sometimes submitted to the reductionistic paradigm with its mechanical way of looking at human persons, while again joining the fight for values which make caring become an act of love and compassion. It is interesting to observe that this development has also been reflected in the development of the concept of "patient" (cf. Eriksson, 1994).

Nurses showed the patient their absolute respect and embraced his dignity. After the 1940's, the medical-technical paradigm became predominant and human dignity was more closely linked to physical attributes, physical strength and health. During the 1960's the idea of human dignity was influenced by the growing social-science paradigm and utilitarian thinking. A person's dignity was determined by how useful and productive he was in society. Today, human dignity is to a large extent linked with economics. A human being, a patient who is economically "unprofitable," has a lower value (cf. Ahlberg, 1951; Bohlin, 1943; Tolonen, 1995).

A human being's vitality and his courage to face life are deeply rooted in his experience of dignity, his own holiness and dignity. To experience holiness, to feel that you are a person of value, gives you the strength and the courage to be neighbor to others and to feel compassion, to love. This is the presumption for being able to care for oneself and for others. A person can violate his own dignity by not being the person he wants to be in his heart.

Human dignity is connected with responsibility and guilt (cf. Braw, 1990). Every person, and maybe especially a suffering person, feels guilt to some extent and condemns himself. A person who does not take on the responsibility for his fellow being feels guilty and thereby he loses some of his own dignity. Guilt and self-condemnation may become unendurable suffering. If a person is allowed to feel that he is loved and that his own dignity is confirmed, he may find the way to reconciliation. According to Lévinas (1982), dignity is the ability to see the other person the way he is and also to be responsible for him. To really see the patient the way he is, perhaps in the middle of hard suffering, means that we take him seriously and that we do not question or reveal him. It also means that we are responsible for the other person's, the patient's, "becoming" in its deepest sense. Every time we meet another person we can, by our attitude, either oppress or confirm the other person, reject or raise him/her to another level of self-respect.

Suffering

Caring which is based on a humanistic paradigm looks upon the patient as a suffering human being, not as a person who is ill. The word "patient" derives from a word for suffering.

Suffering can be explained in many ways, depending on which view is chosen. All suffering, however, has one common denominator; suffering is in some sense a "dying." Suffering is not a feeling or a pain; suffering is more fundamental; it is a state of being (Eriksson, 1992; Lindholm and Eriksson, 1993).

The human being is constantly in a struggle between good and evil, suffering and pleasure. Evil reveals itself in many ways, sometimes getting the better of a person, who may find the suffering unendurable since it is unmotivated, that is, it is in conflict with the sense of goodness, of ethics. This unendurable suffering can make deep wounds in a human being. The suffering person, the patient, needs care that makes the suffering endurable. The human person tries to get away from unendurable suffering by escaping suffering, by entering illness or perhaps denying it, closing it in or becoming immovable to be able to stand it (see Eriksson, 1994).

A human being's ability to suffer is a condition for human growth and sound development. A person's ability to suffer may to some extent have been eroded. Frankl (1987) considers it important to help a suffering person develop the ability to suffer. Through suffering a human being comes in contact with the basic conditions of life, and through suffering a human being can grow to understand the meaning of suffering. Suffering in itself has no meaning, but people can, having lived through suffering, realize that it has a purpose. The ability to suffer is not based on an understanding of why, but on the courage to perceive the actual experience. By all the premature explaining and excusing, we deprive the human being of the possibility to perceive suffering and thereby face suffering and possibly grow through it. There is still danger, nonetheless, that we all too soon give suffering a purpose in order to explain it away, or that we think that suffering can be alleviated by giving it meaning.

The Drama of Suffering

The alleviation of suffering presupposes a recognition and confirmation of suffering in its different shapes and expressions, and an understanding in its deepest sense. Many questions arise as we stand before a suffering human being.

The faces of suffering are so many that suffering becomes intangible and impossible to reach. Still, one of the most important things is to have the courage to admit that suffering exists and to try to reach it. Experiences described by nurses often show that there are ways to understand suffering human beings. A model of suffering in caring has been created through research in a model we called "the drama of suffering." Every instance of suffering is a drama of various degrees of substance and intensity. The drama is formed by "the acts"—confirming, "being" in suffering and "becoming" in suffering (reconciliation or un-reconciliation) (cf. Eriksson, 1992; Lindholm and Eriksson, 1993). The first act is shaped by the extent to which the nurse is able to confirm the patient's suffering. She can either see and accept the suffering, or she can overlook and try to explain it away because she is not able to, or lacks the courage to face it. The second act consists of the nurse's ability to permit suffering, to let the patient remain in suffering, to be able to suffer with him and share in his suffering. The third act could lead to a reconciliation where suffering is part of a new wholeness, but it could also lead to nonreconciliation. Nonreconciliation is a new disappointment to the suffering person. It means not having been received and been confirmed in suffering, which leads to the suffering becoming rigid and sinking deeper and deeper into the human being, not as a natural part of him, but as something strange and frightening.

Suffering and Health

Suffering and love are the deepest and innermost movements of the soul and the spirit and, therefore, they are the most fundamental processes of life and health. Through suffering and love a person is able to grow into a many-sided wholeness and to a deeper holiness, to a wisdom of life and harmony—to become a whole person. By holiness I here mean a person's deep consciousness of his uniqueness and his responsibility as a fellow being.

In its deepest sense, health is an entity through its connection to suffering. If we see suffering as a natural experience of the human person, then suffering also becomes a dimension of health. We know that human suffering of different kinds can become unendurable, reducing our ability to experience human health. A suffering which is unendurable paralyzes us and prevents us from growing. *Health is consistent with endurable suffering.* A person suffering in a way that he finds endurable, can simultaneously experience health. An open question is whether this is always the case.

There is a proverbial phrase that says that a human being cannot appreciate health until he has faced illness. Based on the experience of people, there is a lot of truth in this. It is a matter of awareness. We have found that suffering can give health a meaning when a human being becomes aware of the contrasts and the different possibilities regarding his/her own inner resources.

Regardless of perspective, there is one common denominator in all suffering: a human being is to some extent cut off (reduced) from personal identity and the experience of wholeness. If we look upon health as wholeness (integration), we can see that suffering disturbs this wholeness.

Health is in its deepest sense an ontological concept, that is, it is a question of the individual person's "becoming" and reality (cf. Eriksson and Herberts, 1995; Eriksson ed., 1995). The ontological health model starts with the assumption of health as growing into a deeper oneness toward integration in a person's life. Health is seen as a movement among three different dimensions: health as "behaviour," as "being" and as "becoming." This movement is expressed in a person's experience of different problems, needs or demands. In the dimension of behaviour, health is judged from external objective criteria. In the dimension of being, a person strives for a kind of balance and harmony, and in the dimension of becoming, a person is confronted with suffering. The person strives to reconcile himself with the circumstances of life and to become whole in a deeper dimension of integration. Our studies about suffering showed that suffering can also be perceived in different dimensions, which fall together with the dimensions of health (figure 1).

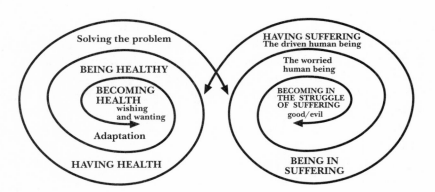

Figure 1. The dimensions of health and suffering.

There is a relation between the different dimensions of health and the strength and extent of the experience of suffering. Suffering can thus be experienced in three dimensions: "suffering as having," "suffering as being" and "suffering as becoming."

1. *To have a suffering* means to be estranged from oneself, one's own inner demands and thus also from one's own possibilities. It means that a person is driven and ruled by external conditions.

2. *To be in suffering* means to look for something more harmonious. The human being often feels anxiety in the middle of something that seems to be a harmonious adaptation. Being is experienced as a state of happiness, harmony and health, at least for some time. However, "to be" is not enough. Stinissen (1990) emphasizes the idea that man, through being, can remain on the periphery of existence and feel relatively harmonious there, but the price he pays is that he denies his innermost self. A person may try to alleviate suffering in a more short-sighted way by means of satisfying his needs. These needs may be satisfied, but man still feels a heightened uneasiness, which sooner or later will urge him on.

3. *To become in suffering* is a struggle between hope and hopelessness, between life and death. When life prevails over death in this struggle it leads to a higher degree of integration, and a person can reconcile himself with his suffering.

Suffering can be unendurable independent of the dimension in which it appears. However, a human being often does not acknowledge suffering when it appears in the dimensions "to have" or "to be." In the dimension "to have," a human being often flees from suffering and tries to make excuses for it. In the dimension "to be," one tries to overcome it by means of satisfying needs to a greater extent. Suffering and health are two different sides to the process of life, they are integrated and always present in a person's life. Depending on the conditions, the human person experiences different degrees of suffering and/or health.

To Find One's Source of Strength

Our fundamental vitality is connected with our ability to absorb nourishment to body, soul and spirit and to be purified.

This ability is related to our ability to feel inclination and disinclination, and to our reason and our ability to see the difference between good and evil. A person's ability to strive is shaped in one's demands, courage and will. It leads to acting and different behaviors, and it also makes up the structure of motives which underlies and rules the whole of health behavior and acting. The structure of motives is determined by the underlying structures of meaning, the whole vitality and our attitude to life.

A human being's archimedic point is a source of strength. The source of strength can be compared with a person's fundamental trust in somebody or something. The strength gives rise to a longing for something that can be described as a thirst (or a hunger). A human being seeks a source where he can slake his thirst. If he finds a source that can slake his thirst, a deeper longing for discovering more of the secret of the source will be born. His thirst increases and he seeks the source once again. This spiral continues and, in the midst of it, new strength is constantly being generated. The spiritual spiral of strength emerges through different movements (figure 2).

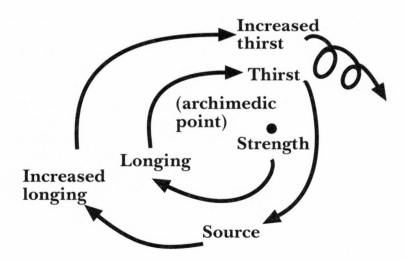

Figure 2. The person's spiritual spiral of strength.

The vitality or the innermost movment, life expression, gives rise to an experience of inclination or disinclination, and the person feels longing. Through perceiving this longing, the person feels thirst. The thirst starts a seeking, or a striving, for the source. The passion (the feeling of inclination at the source) gives rise to an increased longing, and the movement continues toward a higher degree of awareness and a "becoming" as a human being.

The Idea of Caring – The Caring Communion

The idea and origins of caring, the very essence of caring, have come under consideration during the last few years. Caring is the core of nursing (e.g., see Lanara, 1981; Leininger, 1988; Roach, 1987,1992; Watson, 1988). Caring is also the essence of humanity and the basic constitutive phenomenon of human existence. True caring is not a form of behavior, not a feeling or state. It is an ontology, a way of living. It is not enough to "be there"—it is the way, the "spirit" in which it is done; and this is, as I see it, caritative. Caring is a deep human and professional communion. The idea of caring is to alleviate suffering in a spirit of *caritas,* that is, in faith, hope and love. It is compassion upon which true caring is based (Eriksson, 1990, 1992). The human person was born to live in communion with others. Communion is the basis for all humanity (e.g., see Buber, 1963; May, 1983; Tillich, 1952). One logical consequence of this premise is that all forms of caring are variations on human communion.

According to a lexical definition, communion means "the act of sharing," "an intimate relationship with deep understanding" (*Webster's New World Dictionary,* 1988). Caring communion, true caring, occurs when the one caring in a spirit of *caritas* alleviates the suffering of the patient.

Joining in communion means creating possibilities for the other. Lévinas (1982) suggests that considering someone as one's own son implies crossing the border of "the possible." This is a relationship which perceives the other person's possibilities as if they were one's own. It means the ability to shake off the liability of one's own identity and something which is just one's own, and move toward something which is no longer one's own but which belongs to oneself. It is one of the deepest forms of communion. According to Lévinas, it is fatherhood.

Caring communion can be summarized as the art of making something very special out of something less special. Caring communion is a creative act which can imply different forms and contents, but it is characterised by intensity, vitality, openness, possibilities and love.

Caring communion provides a culture that is characterised by warmth, presence, rest, respect, frankness and tolerance. Fundamental entities are care, eye contact, listening, and language. Caring communion is characterised by fighting together, succeeding, being together and going through something together. The situations may vary. There are situations involving a struggle for existence or death, sudden, dramatic, even incurable disease, abortion, etc. There are situations during a regular working day—washing, feeding and caring; or occasions of fear, pain, insomnia, etc. The experience of caring communion does not directly depend on the nature of the situation. The meaning of caring communion can be summarized as the ability to do good for another person. From the patient's point of view, caring communion means the experience of being a subject, of being someone special and important to another person; an experience of someone's responsibility, and willingness to do good for me—such is the experience of good caring. One nurse described it as follows: "...(after the caring situation) she looked like another person, her eyes were clear and she was relaxed...and she had courage to live, had to live in spite of the difficult situation." From the nurse's point of view, there is a meaning in being present, the experience of ministering to the patient, giving something of oneself for the purpose of something very important in the actual situation (Eriksson, 1990).

The Golden Rule

The golden rule is perhaps the most important starting point for care which confirms human dignity. The golden rule, which is regarded as common wisdom, also exists in some form in all great religions of our world, even though it is often ascribed a pure biblical meaning: "Therefore all things whatsoever you would that men should do to you, do you even so to them" (Mt. 7:12). Facing this rule, the human being stands uncovered before the reality of responsibility. He must make a choice in relation to the other person, a choice which forces him to take a stand on how he himself wants to be treated. Buber (1985) relates the rule to the relationship and to human responsibility. A person knows that he shall take care of his brother and, by showing true compassion, bring him into a healing relationship. The golden rule realizes the commandment of love and absolute dignity.

When we invite the other person, we show our fundamental attitude, our basis for values and our inner ethical readiness. According to Kierkegaard (1928), it is the way we invite the other person which reveals how loving we are. The invitation includes a confirmation (cf. Lindström, 1995), and a person knows that he is expected and that he gets a room where he can rest.

I think that we have captured some of the innermost core of caring here. When the nurse shows her respect and true veneration for the patient, she confirms the patient's absolute dignity as a human being. She invites him/her to a caring communion where true compassion and responsibility for the other person give birth to a permissive caring/solicitude. This, in turn, gives the human being/the patient a breathing space, a place for rest and peace, where unendurable suffering can be alleviated. This means that the patient's own vitality and his courage to face life will get a new breeding ground (the nurse breeds in a true culture), and the human being/the patient feels that there are possibilities for a "becoming" towards a new wholeness and holiness.

REFERENCES

Ahlberg, A. 1951. Humanismen (engl. transl. Humanism). Stockholm: Sveriges Kyrkliga Studie-Förlag.

Barbosa da Silva, A. and Eriksson, K. 1991. Vårdteologi (engl. transl. Caring theology). Caring Research 3/1991. The Department of Caring Science, Åbo Akademi, Vaasa.

Berdjajev, N. 1990. Historiens mening: ett försök till en filosofi om det mänskliga ödet (orig. title Smyslistori, Berlin 1923). Skellefteå: Artos.

Bibeln. 1917-års upplaga (The Bible. 1917 ed.).

The Bible. Old and New Testaments, King James Version. 1970 ed. Nashville: Thomas Nelson, Publishers.

Bohlin, T. 1943. Humanismen vid skiljevägen (engl. transl. Humanism at the crossroads). Stockholm: Svenska Kyrkans Diakonistyrelses Bokförlag.

Braw, C. 1990. Skuld och ansvar. Skuld och mänsklig växt (engl. transl. Guilt and responsibility. Guilt and human growth). Stockholm: Verbum.

Buber, M. 1963, 1985. Jag och Du. (orig. title Ich und Du, 1923). Stockholm: Petra bokförlag.

Eliade, M. 1968. Heligt och profant (orig. title Le sacré et le profane). Stockholm: Verbum.

Erikson, E. H. 1959. Identity and the life cycle. New York.

Eriksson, K. 1987. Vårdandets idé (engl. transl. The idea of caring). Stockholm: Almqvist and Wiksell.

——. 1990. Pro caritate—en lägsbestämning av caritativ vård (eng. transl. Caritative caring—a positional analysis). Reports from the Department of Caring Science, Åbo Akademi University.

——. 1992. The alleviation of suffering—the idea of caring. Scandinavian Journal of Caring Sciences 6 (2), 119–23.

——. 1994. Den lidande människan (engl. transl. The suffering human being). Stockholm: Almqvist and Wiksell.

——. red. 1995. Den mångdimensionella hälsan—verklighet och visioner (engl. transl. Multidimensional health—reality and visions). Final report. The Nursing District of the Federation of Municipalities of Vaasa and the Department of Caring Science, Åbo Akademi University.

Eriksson, K. and Herberts, S., 1992. Den mångdimensionella hälsan. En studie av hälsobilden hos sjukvårdsledare och sjukvårdspersonal (engl. transl. Multidimensional health. A study of the health image among nursing leaders and nursing staff). Project report 2. The Nursing District of the Federation of Municipalities of Vaasa and the Department of Caring Science, Åbo Akademi University.

——. 1995. Nursing leaders' and nurses' view of health. Journal of Advanced Nursing, 22, 868–78.

Frankl, V. 1987. Gud och det omedvetna. Psykoterapi och religion (orig. title Der unbewusste Gott: Psychoterapie und religion) Stockholm: Natur och Kultur.

Kierkegaard, S. 1928. Søren Kierkegaards dagbok (engl. transl. Søren

Kierkegaard's diary). Stockholm: Svenska Kyrkans Diakonistyrelses Bokförlag.

Lanara, V. 1981. Heroism as a nursing value: a philosophical perspective. Athens: Sisterhood Evniki.

Leininger, M. 1988. Caring, an essential human need. Detroit: Wayne State University Press.

Lévinas, E. 1982. Etik och oändlighet. Samtal med Philippe Nemo (engl. transl. Ethics and infinity. Conversations with Philippe Nemo). Stockholm: Symposion Bokförlag.

Lindborg, R. 1974. Om människans värdighet (engl. transl. About human dignity). Giovanni Pico della Mirándola. Lund: Vetenskapssocieteten i Lund.

———. 1991. Mänskligt och Naturligt (engl. transl. Human and natural). Stockholm: Norstedts.

Lindholm, L and Eriksson, K. 1993. To understand and alleviate suffering in a caring culture. Journal of Advanced Nursing, 1993, 18, 1354–61.

Lindström, U.Å. 1995. Confirmation has the strength to touch and heal. (Unpubl. manuscript).

May, R. 1983. Den omätbara människan (orig. title The discovery of being: writings of existential psychology). Stockholm: Bonniers Fakta Bokförlag Ab.

Nightingale, F. 1869. Notes on nursing. What it is and what it is not. New York: Dover Publications.

Roach, M. Simone. 1992. The human act of caring: a blueprint for the health professions. (Rev. ed.) Ottawa: Canadian Hospital Association.

Skinner, B. F. 1973. Bortom frihet och värdighet (orig. title Beyond freedom and dignity). Stockholm: Norstedt.

Tillich, P. 1952. Modet att vara till (orig. title The courage to be. Stockholm: Tryckmans Ab.

Stinissen, W. 1990. Natten är mitt ljus (eng. transl. The night is my light). Serie KARMEL, nr 23. Tågarp, Glunslöv: Karmeliterna.

Stott, J. 1986. Meningen med Jesu död (engl. transl. The meaning of the death of Jesus). Örebro: Libris.

Tolonen, L. 1995. Ethics and etiquette in patient care—an idea historical study of how the ethics and the etiquette appear in the professional nursing publication Epione during the years 1908–1965. Licentiate dissertation. The Department of Caring Science, Åbo Akademi University.

Watson, J. 1988. Nursing: human science and human care. a theory of nursing. New York: National League for Nursing.

Webster's new world dictionary. 1988. Third College Edition. New
    York: Simon and Schuster, Inc.

Vonhoff, H. 1962. I kamp mot nöd. Barmhärtighetens historia (engl.
    transl. The struggle against necessity. The story of mercy).
    Stockholm: EFS-förlag Ward Stagebooks.

Photography and Music Give Expression to Caring from the Heart

Kathryn Louise Gramling

Caring is inconspicuous. As such it is devalued and threatened. The power of caring has been obscured in a society which gapes at its absence and glances over its presence. As an expression of the human heart, caring has no neon lights, and it does not seek attention. Modern scientific, technological and bureaucratic systems dwarf manifestations of caring from the heart. Still, caring lives and reveals itself to those who cut through the noise and glare. Caring comes to life in human relationships; there it is formed, displayed and given definition. What methods can we use to bring caring into sharper focus? How can we experience the power of caring so that it may become the prominent force in our work? What can guide us on this path to heart?

My son, David, is a pianist. People comment that his music is soulful and that it "comes from the heart." By this they do not mean that his technique is flawed or that his performance is mindless. The compliment infers that there is a depth and a richness beyond a disciplined mind and skilled fingers in the creation of beautiful sound. David's music is sifted through his heart. The quality of "heart" is honored in the musician.

Health Care and Heart

Expressions from the heart are relegated to the periphery in many arenas of modern life. In our health care systems we are beginning to *feel* what happens when intellect and skill are devoid of heart. The void is experienced when people are asked their insurance carrier before being asked their name, when their arm is being sutured and nobody notices their tears, or when their father is being discussed in objectifying terms within earshot. When someone speaks of "heart" in the health care world it is likely in reference to the coronary care unit, a catheterization or a CPR course. Here the life-saving technical feats are phenomenally executed through fine-tuned skills and minds. But the quality of "heart" expressed by the practitioner through that knowledgeable, skilled performance is neither honored nor understood in a human environment where it should be central.

I suggest that health care professionals turn toward art as a way to recover caring and its power. Art may assist us in centralizing the beautiful caring that is wedged in the crevices of the health care system. To quote Maxine Greene:

> Art has the capacity to enable persons to hear and see what they would not ordinarily hear and see...to disclose the incomplete profiles of the world...to begin with the overtly familiar and transfigure it into something different enough to make those who are awake, hear and see. (1988, p. 133)

In response to the above, I created two projects specifically to illuminate and celebrate the hidden caring in health care. One project involved taking candid photographs of nurses in actual caregiving situations. The other entailed facilitating caring memories through the use of music in teaching learning situations. Both will be described as methods to capture and honor caring. Photography has been utilized effectively as a way to bring caring into focus. Music has served as a means to evoke the caring that is buried in our hearts. One elicits the unseen caring around us; the other becomes a catalyst for the caring within. Both methods have emerged as constructive means of advancing caring in nursing, however, they are relevant for all professionals whose caring work invites further expression and respect.

Expressions of Caring

It is not my intention to define human caring. It is my hope to find it and illuminate it. A human phenomenon as old and as complex as caring seems to beg for multiple meanings and requires a myriad of sources to communicate the richness it evokes. The texture of caring is deep in our being. It is primed and cultivated by our spiritual nature, our ability to extend beyond self and connectedness with others. Caring is exhibited as the manner or mode in which we live authentically in the world as humans persons (Roach, 1992). The capacity of human caring is dependent upon being cared for, and being able to care (Roach, 1992). Both require nurturing by self and others. Each is contingent upon the value we place on the human spirit, our own and that of others.

Personally and professionally, people care because they are human; the manifestations take on various forms depending on occupational skills, experience and purpose (Roach, 1992). Caring also requires knowledge and special knowing (Gaut, 1991). Gaut writes that, "knowledge is seeing through the mind, but knowing is seeing through the heart. Caring as knowledge is transformed to caring as knowing, through reflection; reflection on who we are as human beings, as nurses, as caring persons" (1991, p.1). Frequently caring is trivialized. Comments, such as "all he needs is TLC," often convey a devaluation of the thoughtfulness, preparation and knowledge involved in responsive caregiving. In a small treatise called "On Caring," Mayeroff (1971) reminds us that caring is "not simply a matter of good intentions or warm regard." He writes:

> ...in order to care I must understand the other's needs and I must be able to respond properly to them, and clearly good intentions do not guarantee this. To care for someone I must know many things. I must know for example, who the other is, what his powers and limitations are, what his needs are and what is conducive to his growth; I must know how to respond to his needs, and what my own powers and limitations are. Such knowledge is both general and specific. (p.19)

Professional Caring

Professionally, a strong philosophical foundation of commitment to the other, as well as respectfulness and sensitivity serve as the basis for creating caring in the interpersonal engagement with the client (Watson, 1985). Each experience of caring is unique—uniquely expressed and uniquely received. Yet, like love, caring has universally shared dimensions.

Professional caring is not a substitute for clinical competence; competence and knowledge are presupposed. Caring is partner, spouse, associate to competence in the healing endeavor. Caring is an untapped human resource, rich and diverse, enriching to both the source and the recipient. There are glimpses of its brilliance and transforming power in people's stories. Benner's compilation of reconstructed nursing situations discloses the embedded beauty and the excellence in clinical practice (Benner, 1984). Patients know when a nurse has been caring (Larson, 1984; Clayton, 1989; Essen and Sjoden, 1991). Women who experienced unexpected pregnancy losses reported being cared for when nurses conveyed an understanding of them as individuals, were really "with them," assisted the women in maintaining belief in themselves, and when nurses helped them help themselves (Swanson, 1986). The art of caring in nursing is a transpersonal human activity confirmed in peak experiences by nurse and patients alike (Clayton, 1989). In a phenomenological study of elderly clients and their nurses, a shared sense of elevated sensitivity, exchange of feeling, heightened trust and genuineness was experienced by both parties (Clayton, 1989).

Caring is a concept which is best understood as it is lived in relationships. The experience is shared and heartfelt. Its stories can transform private treasure into public knowledge. Mary Toomey Skinner, a nurse and a speech pathologist, shared a poignant experience she had recently while attempting to "retrain" an elderly woman to safely swallow her food. The patient asked Mary if "people knew when they were about to die." Mary replied that she thought that sometimes people did know and asked the patient if she was worried about dying. The woman responded that she didn't think she would die yet; she "wasn't ready" and talked about her fears of where she would be living and the burden of her care on her sister. Mary and her patient deeply shared the moment. It occurred between spoonfuls of applesauce and it became food for the soul of both.

Rituals and tasks of care situate professionals in compelling intimacies with people at vulnerable times. Caring is qualitatively different than caregiving although the two can be one. Caring involves the sensitive exchange between persons manifested in a touch, a look, or the tone of voice. When the caregiver conveys a "genuine presence" there is a "quality of being in the doing" (Mc Pherson 1987, p.42). This expression of readiness and availability allows meaningful interaction, reciprocity and growth to occur (MacPherson, 1987). To be safe and effective in health care demands competence and knowledge. To be healing, caring must also be present; it opens up the possibilities to give and to receive, to listen and respond; and it directs actions. Here, in relational activities, manifestations of caring are visible.

I believe that the fundamental expression of heart in the health care system is caring and that caring is expressed in the harmony of heart, mind and skill in caregiving. The health care practitioner is particularly positioned to blend humanistic, intellectual and scientific expertise in the service of many. He/she is presented with countless opportunities to enrich caregiving with caring, task with responsivity, mind with heart. However, health care is becoming less relational, more product oriented, mechanistic and technical. Caring is suffering. The health care professional must find ways to protect and nourish the expressions of heart in the system. The alienation of patient and caregiver, colleague and colleague, and patient and family have become so ordinary that we are no longer shocked or outraged by it. The legitimate agenda is so task saturated that the practitioner becomes engulfed in the doing. Investment in the people for whom we care and the expression thereof gets trampled in the rush. The "quality of care" is addressed without attending to the "quality of caring." The heart of the system is marginalized.

It is a tribute to the essential goodness of human beings that caring has survived at all. We must find ways to highlight the presence of caring, rediscover the spirit of our work and awaken the heart of the people in it. There is no beauty in the music for either patient or health care professional until caring takes center stage.

Creating a Visual Story of Caring

Caring needs to be visible. The ability to recognize and acknowledge caring is fundamental in acquiring a sensitivity to caring expressions of others, and for developing the caring capacity within ourselves. I constructed a visual story of nurse-caring as a method of advancing a model of caring with experienced registered nurses in a baccalaureate degree program. With endorsement from agencies, written consent from nurses and patients, opportunities were designed for observation of caregiving encounters. Photographs were taken of interrelational moments. The dignity and integrity of the caregiving situation were insured by close collaboration with clinical nurses and by choosing the least intrusive photographic technique. Over a period of time, patients and nurses seemed to forget the presence of the camera and become less self-conscious. All photographs were candid.

Pictures captured a rich variety of manifestations of caring. Expressions of caring in physical touch, eye-to-eye contact, attentiveness, respect, gentle assistance and overall modes of presence were striking. Glimpses of human connection, sensitivity, intimacy, joy and compassion were disclosed in the images. The photographs made visible an element of professional practice that is overshadowed and taken for granted. Each photograph spoke to me and to each nurse in a very personal way. Many images gave confirmation to the reality of the caring embedded in the practice and rituals of everyday nursing encounters.

Response to the pictorial was very enthusiastic. A variety of exhibits have been held both informally and formally. For example, a collection of photographs was presented at the International Association for Human Caring Conference in 1994 in Portland, Oregon. Exhibits have been held at major health care institutions and in academic settings. Nurses who viewed the photographs felt validated by a pictorial that featured colleagues engaged in caring. Some nurses expressed joy that the caring captured in photographs helped them to refocus on human ideals. Others felt affirmed that caring "doesn't have to be grand" to be caring, that caring can be expressed in small and simple ways. Most photographs triggered nurses' reflections on human interactions and stories from their own lives concerning caring. For example, stories of past patients, of being a patient, of responding with or receiving similar modes of caring were voiced. The photographs also facilitated animated dialogue in the educational setting and served as concrete expressions for exploring the abstract concept of caring. People from outside of health care have applauded the person-centered emphasis portrayed in the photographs as well.

Since my initial efforts in 1992, wide interest and stimulating discussion have encouraged further photographic endeavors including a permanent interdisciplinary pictorial of caring in the Emergency Department of St. Vincent Hospital in Worcester, Massachusetts and a visual caring story at a senior nursing care center. My research in caring continues. A qualitative study using photographs to elicit educators views about caring in nursing is in progress. For me, photography is one vehicle for creating an environment which supports the growth of the caring practitioner. The possibilities of art as an educative tool for personal and professional caring development continue to inspire me.

Art has long been known to provide a powerful voice for people. As creative art, photographs are "experiences captured" (Sontag, 1973). "Each still photograph is a privileged moment, that we can look at again" (p. 12). To view a moment of caring is to share a private treasure. The experience can be savored, understood to some degree and shared by many persons who have known similar moments as either receiver or giver of care. The captive moment, magnified by personal history, is a promise of future caring experiences, and hints of the healing power of human interaction. Numerous images of caring experiences give testimony to the quiet, collective human-to-human contribution of caring. Each photograph can become an opportunity, as Greene says, "a tool for stimulating individuals to reach beyond themselves...to think about what they are doing, to become mindful, to share meaning and to make sense of their lived world" (1988, p.14).

Caring experiences cannot be relegated to happenstance. At least not in the professional realm. Professionals must consciously craft opportunities and circumstances for caring.

Professional education must concentrate on the development of the "capacity to care" through nurturing and "calling forth" the natural propensity to care (Roach, 1987). Instead of a focus on the empirical, scientific path to professional development, nursing and many related health fields need to rethink approaches (Roach, 1992). Lecture is still common in both nursing and medical schools. The study of caring requires "a private journey that nourishes the student's selfhood. The public prescribed journey is not so much educative as instructive learning and leads only to smartness, whereas the private journey leads to wisdom" (Bevis and Watson, 1989, p.32). And "...education for the new age is not about content, it is about soul, about process" (Preface, xi). Caring practitioners require a deepening of knowledge, not only in the mind, but in the human heart. Knowing occurs through empirical, personal, aesthetic, and moral avenues (Carper, 1978). Personal and aesthetic ways of knowing have been underexplored in nursing.

Photographic methods have been used by Darbyshire (1993), who believes that visual media has a liberating potential, in part, because of the productive dialogue which it provokes. He specifically uses photographs to facilitate dialogue and growth in caring. Some advantages that he notes are that photographs can stimulate personal storytelling, highlight ethical concerns, develop interpretive understandings, and relate individual moments to common experiences (Darbyshire, 1993, p.278).

An image of a caring encounter can make the dynamics visible and available to consider in manners that are otherwise inaccessible. Photographs can chronicle visual caring stories that have the potential to resound in the consciousness of others. This extends the personal to the universal. And photographs can serve as reference points for rich dialogue. Photographs which depict the practitioner connecting/being responsive to patients in high technological environments may stimulate self-reflection and discussion about what is limiting and what is not. A photograph can focus on the caring connection, the person-to-person interplay, and bring it to the foreground where it takes center stage. Our visual horizon can be narrowed so that there is opportunity to focus on the one aspect of an otherwise integrated and complex view (Koithan, 1994). In so doing, we become sensitive to and respectful of its power and presence.

Visual processing takes place in the right cerebral hemisphere where creative insights, imaginative thinking and divergent thinking are stimulated (Fergusen, 1992). The creative right brain is underutilized in our concrete linear world. Caring practitioners are going to need to be creative to cope with the rapidly expanding health care environment (Fergusen, 1992). Greene (1988) believes "that caring must be deliberately achieved, as freedom must be achieved.... It is going to take thoughtfulness, courage and desire to do so...an opening of spaces where we can truly care. It is going to take political action...And it may take...poetry and serendipitous visions and music and even painting for the sake of empowering persons to hear and see what is behind the veil" (p. 30).

Evoking Caring Memories and Dialogue with Music

Another method that I have used to achieve illumination of caring from the heart, draws on the power of music. By relaxing the tight controls that the mind imposes on itself and the heart, music can enable people to reexperience forgotten caring moments and animate this foundational source for growth. Music helps the human brain to become more integrated by facilitating right and left brain connections; it may activate the transfer of stored memories across the corpus collosum (Campbell, 1991). Music relaxes, stills the mind, and helps the human being achieve inner quietude (Campbell, 1991). Becoming conscious of past and present caring images can be cultivated by song through a creative reflective process. Music also taps into emotions where caring can be deeply embraced. Very often "we clean up caring" and negate its emotional connections (Smoyak, 1993). Emotions are simply feeling states which can be put in the service of caring, if we so choose.

Music can also help us glimpse the power of caring, our own and that of others. Sometimes, people need encouragement to find their caring stories and to share them. Some need to believe that they have a caring story to tell. Music can encourage this thoughtful work.

Not everyone can turn a shower into an existential experience, but most of us can and do enjoy song. Similar to caring, song belongs to all of us. We are free to consciously embrace its possibilities in our own lives and in our own fashion. Some songs beg for the voice of a lonely tenor; others seem to be designed for harmony and collective power. Using a combined vocal effort in the service of caring reflection, I chose a song called "Shenandoah." It is the kind of song which has lulled people for centuries and into which one's imagination can flow. "Shenandoah" is rich with passion, harmony and longing. Its repetitive gentle rhythm and haunting verse is conducive to personal reflection.

"Shenandoah" is a folk song that may have been a blend of Old Irish and English ballads. The composer is not recorded. Some believe that it was the call of a Missouri River raftsman who was celebrating his love for a Native American princess. Others think that frontiersman and the crews of early clipper ships in the Atlantic sang this slow rhythmic chant during shipboard tasks (*The American Heritage Songbook*, 1969, p. 40).

My first experience of "Shenandoah" was in elementary school. As one of fifty fourth graders arranged in rows, separated by gender and ordered by height, I struggled to bring the ballad to life to the satisfaction of Sister Mary Catherine. It was difficult to raise my voice with glee from a sitting position at my desk with hands folded. I heard "Shenandoah" again four years ago, in a lovely old symphony hall in Worcester, Massachusetts. Late and harried, I was rethinking my day when youthful voices resonated from all sides of the auditorium. My eyes watered, my hair follicles constricted, and my heart warmed with lovely thoughts. The first verse reads:

> O Shenandoah, I long to see you,
> away ye rolling river
> O Shenandoah, I long to hear you,
> A way, we're bound a-way,
> Cross the wide Missouri!

The song is mine in spirit now, although I share its a cappella version by the 1994 Massachusetts Central District High School Chorale in the classroom as a method of teaching/learning caring in nursing.

For example, in small group work, I have found this song to provide a context and a vehicle for evoking and sharing personal stories of past and present caring. After spending time relaxing and focusing thoughts on caring, students are guided to recall caring memories and experiences from their personal or professional past. The song "Shenandoah" is used during the exercise, as a vehicle to soothe, relax and decrease anxieties. Students are invited to recall images of past caring moments and to reexperience them if they wish. After two full renditions of the musical score, students are guided from relaxation to attentive presence. Experiences are shared voluntarily. For those caring images shared with the group, there is discussion of the meaning and the power of the caring memory. Students are usually able to perceive clear images of caring and associated feelings. Classmates affirm each other's unique experiences and hear a range of manifestations of caring.

Arndt (1992) suggests that telling stories of caring will help reveal the hidden practices which may be too ordinary or everyday to see. "Nursing stories naturally serve as an exquisite source for understanding the content of nursing" (Boykin and Schoenhofer, 1991, p. 246). Stories alert us to the commonalties as well as the uniqueness in caring situations (Boykin and Schoenhofer, 1991). Recollection of past experiences can inform and create possibilities for the present (Arndt, 1992). A caring consciousness is not an outright gift; it is a process which must be achieved with effort and mindfulness. Noddings (1984) and Roach (1992) believe that early experiences of caring and being cared for are foundational to the development of caring and the development of the caring person. All of us have experienced caring moments, as both a giver and a receiver. As a uniquely human quality, each of us has the capacity to care, but it needs to be brought forth and nurtured (Roach, 1987, 1992). Students of nursing have enjoyed the use of "Shenandoah." They find that relaxing and imaging to the song assists them in generating insights from forgotten caring engagements. Personal caring images are created from individual experiences. The power of caring moments is experienced, re-experienced and communicated among colleagues Music becomes a vehicle to expose the reservoir of caring deep within. I believe that these self-generated manifestations of caring are more likely to nurture the development of the caring practitioner than would abstract generalizations. Moore's (1992) words seem particularly appropriate here:

> The point of art is not simply to
> express ourselves, but to create
> an external/concrete form in
> which the soul of our lives can
> be evoked and contained.
> (P. 302)

Concluding View

"Caring" is a word which is often used and is less frequently attended to in health care. Caring is noticeable when absent yet rarely designed in health care services. Caring has been subsumed, overwhelmed by a technical, disease-oriented model of care. More recently, caring is endangered by economic and bureaucratic decisions. Glimpses of nurses' expressions of caring are evident in photographs in spite of the situational barriers to doing so. Images of caring experiences are readily evoked through music and reflection. These two creative methods access an enduring desire to care by experienced nurses in a rapidly dehumanizing environment. There is caring evident around us and within us. Its natural force and power warrant cultivation and reverence. Professionals need to make a conscious choice for caring and then decide what is needed in order to practice in caring ways. There is an urgent need for a redirection of energy and resources in engineering and sustaining professional caring manifestations. Caring cannot be mandated, it can only be nourished through personal and professional development. We cannot continue to leave caring to chance. It must be consciously orchestrated.

My oldest son is a third year medical student; he wants to be a "country doctor." One of the greatest accolades that he can attain is if it is said of him that "his work is soulful...that it comes from his heart." Like his interdisciplinary colleagues he will have to struggle to assert heart in health care. For all those who practice with him in the twenty-first century, may caring competence be the expectation, not the exception. And may we support them as they strive to advance the soul as well as the science of health care.

REFERENCES

Arndt, M. J. (1992). Caring as everydayness. *Journal of Holistic Nursing,* 10(4), 285–93.

Benner, P. (1984). *From Novice to Expert; Excellence and Power in Clinical Nursing.* Menlo Park, Calif.: Addison-Wesley.

Bevis, E., and Watson J. (1989). *Toward a Caring Curriculum: A New Pedagogy for Nursing.* New York: National League for Nursing Press.

Boykin, A. and Schoenhofer, S. (1991). Story as link between nursing practice, ontology and epistemology. *IMAGE: Journal of Nursing Scholarship,* 23,(4), 245–48.

Campbell, D. (1991). *Music: Physician for Times to Come.* London, England: Quest Books.

Carper, B. (1978). Fundamental patterns of knowing in nursing. *Advances in Nursing Science,* 1(1), 13–23.

Clayton, G., (1989). Research testing Watson's theory: the phenomena of caring in an elderly population. In Riehl-Sisca, J.P. (Ed.). *Conceptual Models for Nursing Practice* (3rd ed.). Norwalk, Conn.: Appleton and Lange.

Darbyshire, P.(1993). Understanding caring through photography. In N. Diekelmann and M. Rather (Eds.), *Transforming RN Education: Dialogue and Debate* (pp.274–89). New York: National League for Nursing Press.

Essen, L. and Sjoden, P. (1991) (Perceived Occurrence and importance of caring behaviors among patients and staff in psychiatric, medical and surgical care. *Journal of Advanced Nursing,* 21(266–76).

Fergusen, L. (1992). Teaching for creativity. *Nurse Educator.* 17(1), 16–19.

Gaut, D. (1993). *Human Caring Newsletter.* International Assoc. for Human Caring: Beaverton, Oregon: October, (p.1).

Greene, M. (1988). *The Dialectic of Freedom.* New York: Teachers College, Columbia University.

Koithan, M.,(1994). The seeing self: photography and storytelling as a health promotion methodology. In Chinn and Watson (Eds.), *Art and Aesthetics in Nursing (pp. 247–62)*. New York: National League for Nursing Press.

Larson, P.(1984). Important nurse caring behaviors perceived by patients with cancer. *Oncology Nursing Forum*, 11(6).

Mayeroff, M. (1971).*On Caring*. New York: Harper and Row.

McPherson, P. (1987). The quality of being expressed as doing. *The Australian Journal of Advanced Nursing*. 5,(1). 38–42.

Moore, T. (1992) *Care of the Soul*. New York: Harper Perennia.

Noddings, N. (1984). *Caring: A Feminine Approach to Ethics and Moral Education*. Berkeley: University of California Press.

Roach, S. (Rev. ed., 1992). *The Human Act of Caring : A Blueprint for the Health Professions* (Rev.ed). Ottawa: Canadian Hospital Association Press.

Smoyak, S. (1993). Strategies for implementing the dreams in nursing. *Journal of Nursing Education*, 32 (1), 5–11.

Sontag, S. (1973). *On Photography*. New York: Farrar, Straus and Girou.

Swanson, K. (1986). Caring in the instance of unexpected early pregnancy loss. *Topics in Clinical Nursing*, 8(2), 37–46.

——. (1993) Nursing as informed caring for the well-being of others. *IMAGE: Journal of Nursing Scholarship*, Winter, 25(4), 252–357.

The American Heritage Songbook. (1969). New York: American Heritage Publishing Co. Inc.

Watson, J.(1985). *Nursing: Human Science and Human Care*. New York: Appleton Century Crofts.

Transcultural Spirituality: A Comparative Care and Health Focus

Madeleine Leininger

If nurses are to work effectively with people of diverse cultures, they must understand their own cultural heritage but also the beliefs, values, and lifeways of people who are different from them yet similar in some respects. The spiritual and religious dimensions however are the highest order to understand and yet most difficult to know fully the essence, soul, and spiritual genuineness of human beings.

In the long history of human existence, culture with its religious and spiritual values, expressions, and meanings has been a powerful force to guide human actions, health and well-being. Individual and group beliefs about the meaning of life, existence, illness and death have generally been buttressed in spiritual and religious values and ideas. Transcultural spirituality with its special meanings, symbols and practices is a most useful guide to caring and healing modalities, or to facing illness, disability and death. It is a phenomenon that only in recent decades nurses and other health care providers are beginning to study systematically in order to discover the meaning and expressions of comparative dimensions of human spirituality as a caring and health force.

In this chapter, the author defines and discusses transcultural spirituality with a focus on caring and health. The importance of understanding comparative spirituality that is largely embedded in religious and related general cultural beliefs and values is addressed. Some examples of transcultural meanings, symbols and lifeways of specific cultures are presented to help nurses realize that both diversities and some universalities exist with regard spiritual caring which influence the health and well-being of people. The author takes the position that nurses need to become knowledgeable about comparative transcultural spirituality in order to guide nursing care practices that are meaningful and congruent with the cultural orientations, beliefs and lifeways of people. Currently, the comparative perspective of spiritual care is missing in nursing education and practice, which greatly limits the nurse in providing effective caring and healing practices. There is also a prevailing assumption that spirituality or spiritual care is similar or alike among all peoples without realizing that there are diverse meanings and practices among human groups. Furthermore, there is a tendency for nurses to assume that spirituality and religion are one and the same phenomenon. The lack of transcultural education, research and practices has contributed to these developments.

Status of Spiritual Care in Nursing

During the past two decades there has been a growing interest in spiritual care which has largely been stimulated by the study and interest in human caring and some in transcultural nursing (Carson, 1989; Lane, 1987; Leininger, 1970, 1977, 1981, 1986, 1995; Horn, 1990; Ray, 1989; Roach, 1992; Watson, 1985).

The comparative transcultural meanings and practices have been neglected by many nurses who have not been prepared in transcultural nursing. Granted, some nurses acknowledge and discuss Judeo-Christian ideas of spirituality with religious beliefs, but the *comparative* cultural dimensions regarding many other religions and spiritual expressions are often neglected in the nursing literature. There are also nurses who make claims that nurses "have always historically addressed and responded to the spiritual needs of patients," but this is questionable when nurses were devoid of cultural spiritual knowledge about specific cultures. Recently in Barnum's (1995) stimulating article on spirituality in nursing she used the subtitle "Everything Old is New Again," reaffirming the above myth. Nonetheless, Barnum offers some valuable perspectives about spirituality, however, but the cultural dimensions are limitedly explored. This makes it very difficult to understand how everything is "old and new again" with regard to the spiritual needs of clients from a worldwide perspective. For without comparative knowledge of spiritual care from a cultural perspective, the meanings and practices to clients may differ and limit the nurse meeting their spiritual needs. One can only predict that the nurse's own personal and unicultural ideas about spirituality have largely guided nursing interpretations and actions.

From the author's extensive transcultural nursing observations and practices in the past four decades, it is clear that the spiritual needs of clients have been evident in nurse-client encounters; however, culture-specific care has not prevailed. Nonetheless, since the advent of transcultural nursing with a caring focus, more nurses are becoming aware of differential spiritual care which needs to be studied systematically and used in culture-specific ways (Leininger, 1970, 1978, 1986, 1991, 1995). The use of qualitative research methods has also been extremely helpful to discover covert dimensions of spiritual care in different cultures. It was the combined focus on transcultural care and qualitative research beginning in the early 1960s that enabled nurses to study the spiritual and religious systems of diverse cultures. Today, transcultural nurses realize there are differences among western and nonwestern cultures of how they know, interpret and practice spirituality and caring. The emic (insider's) and etic (outsider's) views of spirituality and religion within a cultural holistic perspective have been studied for the first time and have greatly increased nurses' cultural knowledge base. These transcultural nursing research studies focused explicitly on spiritual care and religious forms, meanings and interpretations from the people's perspectives. This knowledge helped to reduce ethnocentrism, ethical conflicts and cultural imposition practices related to spiritual and religious nursing practices (Leininger, 1970, 1978, 1990a, 1990b, 1995; McFarland, 1994; Ray, 1989; Rosenbaum, 1989; Stasiak, 1984; Wenger, 1988; and others). As a consequence, new or different perspectives of transcultural spirituality begin to be known in nursing. The search for comparative spiritual meanings and practices continues to be extremely important in order to advance nursing knowledge and practices and to provide culturally congruent spiritual care.

It has been the theory of culture care diversity and universality which has helped nurses to go beyond their personal, local and ethnocentric views (Leininger, 1978, 1988, 1991, 1995). This major nursing theory has been focused on the culture's values, religious, philosophical, educational and other dimensions bearing upon spiritual care. Actually it was the first nursing theory that focused on cultural spiritual care dimensions with the use of the Sunrise Model and diverse factors influencing spiritual care and health. The theory has been enormously helpful to move beyond the biomedical model of focusing primarily on the mind and body to that of searching for comparative holistic (including spiritual) care of specific cultures. Many undergraduate and graduate students have often said to the author: "The theory of culture care diversity and universality made me aware for the first time in my profession that spiritual beliefs and care differ among people. It made me reexamine my beliefs and what I had been taught in nursing and at home."

Most importantly, the transcultural care theory and the ethnonursing research method have led to a new paradigm in nursing with new meanings and expressions of spiritual caring within and between specific cultures. Nurses have discovered that spiritual care is largely culturally constituted and takes on meaning within a cultural context. Comparative caring with a holistic perspective continues to challenge nurse-clinicians, scholars, ethicists and philosophers of nursing as the new paradigm is being used by nurse-educators researchers, and practitioners. Accordingly, nurses are incorporating the spiritual caring dimensions from a comparative cultural perspective in their nursing. They are becoming aware of their own personal biases and are discovering new ways to provide cultural-specific spiritual care with clients of diverse cultures (Leininger, 1974). At the same time, nurses continue to search for what is universal and diverse about spiritual care. Ethical and moral aspects from a transcultural comparative stance are also being explored as the nurses see and hear different beliefs and practices regarding spirituality and religion that bear upon nursing care. Unquestionably, during the past four decades, the transcultural nursing movement has greatly expanded nurses' traditional knowledge base to a comparative one with ways to provide culturally congruent, specific and responsible care. The latter is the goal of the theory of culture care diversity and universality (Leininger, 1988, 1991, 1995). The transcultural nursing paradigm and the use of theory of culture care have also encouraged nurses to reexamine the traditional mind-body-spirit focus to that of multiple dimensions of care, that is, philosophical, religious, spiritual, economic, technologic, kinship, language, education and specific cultural values within the people's ethnohistorical and environmental contexts (Leininger, 1991, 1995).

Most importantly, transcultural nursing with a care focus challenged past theoretical and narrow views of human behavior. Spirituality as a psychological state or a biomedical condition has been challenged as too studied, limiting the grasp of the world of the client and especially spiritual and religious systems. The new paradigm challenges nurses who view spirituality from a physical perspective or an energy field or force. Such psychological and physical views of spirituality are often not congruent with the beliefs and values of specific cultures as they are too much "in the body," or too materialistic. Beliefs about the power, mercy and healing of a supreme being, God, Jesus, or other outside intellectual beings or spirits have to be considered. Beliefs in a supreme or superior being such as God or other supernatural forces are prevailing beliefs in many cultures in the world. Hence, Longway's (1970) view of the nurse restoring power by supplying energy as a spiritual force would be difficult for many cultures to uphold. Furthermore, Quinn's (1992) view of the nurse as a healing environment and as an energetic healing force for therapy would also be difficult for many non-Anglo-Americans to accept. Likewise Watson's transpersonal mind, body and spirit perspective is difficult for some nurses and clients to value and understand, as spirituality is more than between persons with subjective and intersubjective psychological feelings (Watson, 1985). The cultural dimensions have to be considered. In general, most nursing theories have failed to incorporate the transcultural comparative data of human cultures in caring processes. Transcultural spiritual care remains largely unexplored when one considers the many diverse meanings, forms, values, functions and expressions of spiritualism, spirituality and human caring within complex cultures. It is the diversities and universalities of spiritual care that remain extremely important if nurses are to provide spiritual care to clients of different cultures and make claims of providing this service.

Definition of Terms and Inferential Meanings

Before proceeding further, some general definitions of transcultural spirituality, religion, spiritual care and transcultural nursing are in order. The following definitions have been formulated by the author drawing upon transcultural nursing research and from selected theological, anthropological and philosophical perspectives of these transculturally based constructs.

> **Transcultural spirituality** refers to diverse and similar modes of knowing or experiencing a life force, power, or transcendental inspiration from a source outside or within a person (or group) that gives meaning, explanations, connectedness and a way of understanding one's beliefs, values, lifeways and place in the universe with a supernatural being or life force.

> **Spiritual caring** refers to those explicit acts, attitudes and modes of helping individuals and groups that are largely derived from the emic cultural world of clients that give inspiration, meaning, unity (external and internal), and become a vital source for healing, health, or state of resignation for living or dying. (Leininger, 1978, 1990a)

> **Spirituality** is a connectedness to and a unity relationship with a life force, a supreme or supernatural being with symbolic referents that gives meaning and guides one's beliefs, hopes and actions.

> **Religion** refers to an institutionalized or a formal system of beliefs (dogma) with rituals and practices to worship God

and/or a supernatural being with fervent faith and devotion. (Leininger, 1978, 1995; Merriam Webster, 1994, p. 619)

Transcultural nursing refers to a formal area of study and practice focused on comparative cultural care (caring) values, beliefs and practices of individuals and groups of similar or different cultures with the goal of providing culture-congruent and specific nursing care practices to promote the health or well-being of clients or to help them face unfavorable human conditions, illness or death in culturally meaningful ways. (Leininger, 1978, 1995)

From the above definitions, there are several important ideas and principles to consider about transcultural spiritual care as well as myths and misconceptions. Hence the following explicative statements are offered for reflection and research purposes.

1. Religion and spirituality may not be the same phenomena (Haviland, 1993; Kottak, 1991; Williams, 1990). Spirituality may go beyond religion with broad philosophical and epistemic meanings and interpretations or with a very specific narrow interpretation.
2. Spirituality generally transcends the biological, mechanical and material dimensions of knowing and explaining one's existence or condition.
3. Spirituality is a life-giving and unity force which gives in-depth meanings, relationships and/or connectedness to others from a supernatural or a supreme being or another source.
4. From a transcultural perspective the most universal feature of spirituality is that it is usually a source of hope, consolation, love, healing, renewal, inspiration and power with special meanings that generally comes from God or an external source and it is incorporated into one's lifeways or to serve others.
5. Spiritual caring (care) may come from religious beliefs and practices, but it may also come from other sources that are held to be sacred, valued, or an inspirational life source. Generally spirituality comes from a higher and outside source such as from God, saints, supernaturals or from spiritually-oriented persons or symbols that serve as exemplars or role models of

ways of living to attain one's purpose in life or to honor and
respect a higher being. Most importantly, spiritual forces that
are caring are restorative and health-promoting. They may also
bring about personal justice, protection and a balance in living
as one prays, reflects, meditates or seeks reconciliation and
connectedness to another.

6. From a transcultural nursing perspective, there are diverse
   and universal forms, meanings and expressions of spiritual
   caring and spirituality that necessitate systematic study in
   order to be knowledgeable about spiritual caring (Leininger,
   1970, 1978, 1991, 1995).
7. Spiritual caring may not be unique to nursing but in the practice of nursing. It is often unique in nursing because of the
   holistic, direct and continuous caring ways that spirituality can
   become therapeutic in nurse-client relationships.
8. Spiritual caring with the sick, disabled, dying or persecuted
   takes on special meanings with clients, and guides nurses to
   respect and understand clients' spiritual needs.

These above ideas and principles help the nurse to reflect upon
the definitions and to understand spiritual caring from a transcultural comparative perspective. Unquestionably, as nurses
expand their thinking and develop a comparative stance about
spirituality, spiritual referents and religious ideas in several cultures, their sensitivity, understanding and competence will
become evident. Learning about religious and spiritual rituals,
supernaturals, symbols, sacred places, and beliefs from different
cultures is important. The nurse will also discover that in some
cultures, spirituality may emanate from animals, trees, stones,
mountains, dreams and from diverse inanimate objects.
Nonhuman forces may be extremely significant to clients, as they
serve as animating life forces to guide, protect, console or attain
power to live, survive or regain health. Many diverse spiritual
human and nonhuman life forces exist transculturally, but one
needs to discover and understand them from the local people living in their familiar cultural contexts. Let us turn now to specific
cultural variations of spirituality with examples.

Cultural Variations of Spirituality

In practically all cultures in the world, one will find some variations on the meanings, forms, expressions and interpretations of spirituality (Kottak, 1991; Leininger, 1990a, 1990b; Oswalt, 1986; Williams, 1990). Transculturally speaking, spirituality may be stimulated by or emanate from both outside and inside sources. Spirituality coming from a supreme being—God, Jesus, saints, special symbols, inanimate objects or from unknown sources—exists and varies in different functions and uses. In some cultures, spiritual forces are feared as they are held to be extremely powerful. These forces are usually external to the person and may be gender related (Hsu, 1981). Often males may have great supernatural power, as observed with Native Americans. But sometimes females are believed to have great spiritual power through their prayers, actions and petitions in getting help for and from others. Female spiritualists may go into dance trances, as found in Latin America. The use of supernatural or spirit power can be feared or held in great respect. Generally spiritual life power is gradually assimilated or incorporated into one's daily lifeways to heal, restore, console or gain control of oneself.

Still another important idea is that spirits and spirituality may be located in different parts of the body. For Christians and those of Islam, the spiritual force or soul is located in the heart. Catholics and other Christians often pray to fill their hearts with God's love or strength, or to protect and love others. Devotion to the Immaculate Heart of Mary and the Sacred Heart of Jesus are a few examples of the heart and spirituality. There are some cultures who view spirituality as residing in the total human body with spiritual connectedness to other persons, such as with Melanesian cultures in the Pacific Islands. Still another important idea is that spirit or spirituality may be located in the mind, body and/or brain, and there are many spirits in the head, as found with Vietnamese. But there are cultures in which spirituality is located and understood to exist outside the body, ruling the earth, water and cosmos.

When spirits or spiritual life forces roam about the earth, this is very unusual and very frightening to the people. It requires that the people be cognizant of their cultural taboos and watch their behavior so that they do not offend the spirits. In these cultures there are often many folk tales of how the people learn to capture roaming spirits and get power from them. In some cultures if one does not have spiritual power, one can become very ill and die or have great misfortunes come to him/her. The nurse needs to be knowledgeable about these differences among different cultures and to recognize the sources of spirituality and how it can influence the individual's, group's or community's health, illness and general well-being.

From the author's study of the Gadsup of the eastern highlands of New Guinea, the Gadsup hold that spirituality and the life (spirit) force comes from their deceased ancestors (Leininger, 1978, 1993, 1995). They believe that it is the spiritual life essence of their deceased kinsmen whom they honor and who will protect and help them. In time of crisis or general need, they ask their ancestors for help and especially for moral and ethical guidance in their daily lives. Protective spiritual care is sought to protect the villagers from external enemies. Gadsup spiritual life essence helps them explain and know about unusual day and night happenings. They respect their ancestors by not breaking established cultural taboos or values that their ancestors upheld. In general, the Gadsup ancestors become a spiritual, ethical and moral guide to villagers in their daily lives. The nurse would need to be knowledgeable about the Gadsup concept of spirituality and be attentive to specific Gadsup cultural taboos of the ancestors that could lead to illness and death if not upheld. In recent decades, Christian religious leaders mainly from Lutheran, Catholic, and Seventh Day Adventist groups have tried to change Gadsup beliefs, but have found it difficult because of the people's beliefs and respect for their deceased ancestors. But there are some Gadsup who have accepted Christian concepts of spirituality as Jesus, God or a supreme being. In general, nurses functioning with the Gadsup would have to asses the spiritual and religious beliefs of individuals and families in order to understand their two-world "religious and spiritual interests and needs."

In the Pacific Islands, there are several Polynesians who believe that the animals, mountains and rocks have spiritual power, but especially mammals such as sharks. Sharks are sources of strong spiritual power—power which can guide, inspire and protect the people from harm. Polynesians perform rituals and work hard to capture shark power in their sea-hunting efforts. This power is needed to help the people stay well and to protect them from evil, sickness and external dangers.

In the Christian cultures with the belief in a supreme being, saints, Jesus, Mary and Joseph, spirituality is believed to flow from God's love and mercy. Hence, prayers, petitions and Christian sacramental acts are important means to become and remain spiritual as well as to fulfill God's will. Christian spirituality means being closely connected to God's will and to follow Christ's teaching, which in turn can bring protection, special blessings, healing and salvation. Judeo-Christian spirituality is inherent in and supported by religious beliefs and practices. Religious beliefs and teachings from the Bible give meaning to life, suffering, death, sickness, evil and misfortunes. Christians recognize a higher supreme being (God) who becomes a model and inspiration for people to perfect their lives, do good and gain eternal salvation. Unity and a closeness to God require prayers, faith and doing God's will through spiritual acts.

In China and many southeast Asian cultures, one finds quite different spiritual beliefs and practices (Hsu, 1981; Kottak, 1991). Confucianism serves as a philosophy of humanity and a spiritual guide for proper living in order to maintain social order, peaceful living and harmony (Leininger, 1995, p. 541). Humanistic virtues as a philosophy of living embraces spirituality as a humanistic endeavor and lifeway. Likewise, Taoism is a philosophy and worldview that supports balance, harmony, inner strength between nature and human beings. It is different from Confucianism, as one must transcend human society and gave emphasis to "the way" or "the path" as an ultimate reality. Taoism as well as Buddhism includes beliefs in the Yang as a creative and demanding force and the Yin as a recessive, receptive and hidden force (Hsu, 1981; Leininger, 1995; Major, 1989). These spiritual concepts are essential for nurses to provide spiritual care in order for southeast Asians to attain and maintain their health or well-being.

Buddhism was founded by Siddhartha Gautama (between 500 and 480 B.C.) and after the time of Confucianism and Taoism. It is a religion with explicit doctrines and ways to reach and maintain a "good life." Spirituality is an integral part of Buddhistic religious beliefs and action modes. Buddhism has many specific beliefs which the nurse would need to study in order to assist clients of this faith. Knowledge of these beliefs in the power of Buddha, along with respect for people going to their shrines for healing and preparing for reincarnation are important for the spiritual care of many southeast Asians.

For Native Americans residing in North America, the traditional and universal spiritual belief among approximately seven hundred Native Americans is focused on the "Great Spirit." The Great Spirit is a supernatural being that has tremendous power over humans and over all living things in one's environment. In the past, young males traditionally went into the forest or into their natural environment on a "spiritual quest" in order to obtain spiritual power from the Great Spirit and to become a shaman (Kottak, 1991; Williams, 1990). To become a shaman who could heal, protect and help people regain their health required knowledge of folk beliefs and a ritualized socialization process. The quest for spiritual inspiration and power was an ideal goal for many men in the culture. A psychological and culturally-oriented spiritual state was essential in order to become an effective and respected shaman healer and a powerful spiritual counselor balancing forces between man and his environment. Still today many Native American nations emulate and believe in the Great Spirit, Mother Earth, and the sources of spirituality from the four points on earth. While there are slight variations among Native Americans, the universal spiritual belief in the Great Spirit has guided most Native Americans in maintaining their spiritual well-being and health. Specific caring ways have been identified to support Native American spiritual beliefs and practices (Horn, 1995; Oswalt, 1986; Phillips and Lobar, 1995). In recent decades, several transcultural nurses have studied the meanings of Native American spiritual caring lifeways (Horn, 1990, 1995; Leininger, 1978, 1995; Phillips and Lobar, 1995; and others) and are applying this knowledge in care practices.

Although many more cultures could be cited to illustrate the diversity in spirituality and religious systems, the above examples show the importance of being knowledgeable about cultural variations. Nurses are encouraged to read about different cultures to increase their knowledge of transcultural variations and similarities in spiritual care among many cultures in the world (Andrews and Boyle, 1995; Dobson, 1991; Leininger, 1978, 1995; Oswalt, 1986; Williams, 1990). Such knowledge is essential if nurses are to understand and provide spiritual care to people of diverse cultures. For without knowledge and use of diverse spiritual and religious beliefs and values, nursing care will not be effective and clients will be deprived of essential care. Moreover, some unfavorable responses or unfavorable outcomes may occur due to lack of culture-specific spiritual care. The universal aspect among cultures is the belief in a spiritual or supreme being that is more powerful than themselves. Cultures rely on supernaturals for spiritual guidance, health, renewal and inspiration. Cultures use different linguistic terms about spirituality and their interpretations may vary as well. The roles, functions and outcomes of spiritual leaders and followers also vary. Most importantly, spiritualism is something which requires in-depth knowledge of the culture and a study of specific rituals and beliefs.

Spiritual Illness and Health

This chapter would not be complete without consideration of spiritual illness and health from a transcultural perspective. Generally, spiritual illness comes from spiritual conflicts between external and internal forces or from the absence (or neglect) of not upholding certain beliefs and practices in a culture. Spiritual illnesses can be due to sin or evil or by not following supreme being expectations. Cultural illnesses may come from professional and client conflicts that reflect a violation of cultural taboos and practices at home or in the hospital contexts. Professional staff may unintentionally impose ideas that are counter to the client's spiritual beliefs which can lead to illness and sometimes death of the client. Mashiba (1995) talks about the nurse who failed to recognize the South African medicinemen, herbalists or midwives and their role in spiritual healing. Or nurses may fail to recognize an evil spell and not be comfortable having traditional spiritual healers participate in the caring process, as found especially in South African traditional lifeways.

When a client or family becomes ill, the nurse needs to consider first that spiritual cultural factors may have precipitated or led to the illness. The author recalls a young man who was depressed and wanted to die. He said he had violated God's ways too much and could never regain his mercy. This man needed spiritual help from the nurse and priest to help him regain his spiritual well-being and health. Pills and psychological treatments were of limited help, as his problem was a breakdown in his relationship with God. The nurse offers spiritual care by the use of cultural knowledge and using caring strategies useful to clients. Effective spiritual healing necessitates the integration of cultural values and beliefs into the caring process, and the use of local healers when indicated. For if spiritual healing does not occur, clients will remain ill, experience suffering or even die. Spiritual prayers, rites, rituals and healing modes are needed in caring that includes cultural healers' participation.

Since spiritual beliefs and practices are often complex, abstract and difficult for nurses to understand, especially with regard to nonwestern traditional practices and beliefs, the nurse should seek mentors prepared in transcultural nursing and indigenous constraints. Western nurses should not totally rely on their own personal and religious beliefs to deal with unknown spiritual differences of cultures. Nurses should first consider the clients' spiritual needs rather than always looking first for physical symptoms and diseased conditions to explain and treat illness conditions. In nonwestern cultures, the author has noted that spiritual leaders use nonphysical approaches first and then seek western or professional healers and treatments as the last resort (Leininger, 1991, 1995). And since spirituality is often buttressed in religious and other cultural beliefs, the nurse needs to study the religious beliefs in order to respond appropriately to clients and to understand them. Accurate care assessments take into account spiritual and religious factors. It is also important to realize this even though these spiritual and religious beliefs may be strange or unknown to the nurse and other health professionals.

To become effective in spiritual caring, the nurse first studies specific cultures with focus on spiritual and religious beliefs, rituals and practices from a caring perspective. A broad holistic perspective of the client's culture is important in order to discover the meanings and nature of spirituality. The Sunrise Model and theory of culture care can be of great assistance (Leininger, 1991). Listening to and responding to the religious beliefs, values and lifeways about spiritualism of the client and family can be enormously helpful to the nurse's understanding. Care as the essence and dominant focus of nursing means that the nurse needs to focus on the subtle, covert or unspoken aspects of the clients' spiritual- and religious-care beliefs and needs, and then use these discoveries in nursing-care actions and decisions (Leininger, 1981, 1984). The incorporation of spiritual care with other aspects of nursing is an essential and creative endeavor. The three modes of providing spiritual care in the theory of culture care can help to insure that spiritual care will become part of nursing care practices (Leininger, 1991, 1995).

It is the author's position that nurses should not leave spiritual care to priests, rabbis, ministers or special pastors. Nurses are responsible for the spiritual care of clients in order to promote clients' health and well-being. Of course religious ministers and indigenous spiritual healers have their unique roles and responsibilities and must fulfill them. It is the nurse who is in a special position to provide spiritual care to clients around the clock, in times of crisis, or for special needs as a direct and intimate care provider. As nurses work with religious and spiritual healers and understand their roles, they can identify their special contributions (Hall and Hilreth, 1993).

Today there are priests, rabbis, nurses and other health providers who have had very limited formal preparation in comparative religious systems and spiritual beliefs, thus limiting their ability to care for clients and their families in spiritual and religious ways. Until this situation is remedied, transcultural nurses and others who have been prepared in comparative spiritual care can be of assistance to others. While transcultural nurses have led other professional disciplines to investigate the spiritual and religious care dimensions and use findings in their practice, still there are many cultures yet to study and document changes in the culture. While anthropologists have long studied religious systems and spirituality aspects, only a few have been interested in human caring and its relationship to the health and well-being of people of particular cultures (Haviland, 1993; Hsu, 1981; Geertz, 1973). Nevertheless, a general interest in religious and spiritual dimensions is growing in the last decade.

A recent development in nursing has been the parish nurse and pastoral chaplains who work in hospitals and health agencies or out of church organizations. Unfortunately, very few of these nurses have had preparation in transcultural nursing, which again limits their ability to provide spiritual care to clients of diverse cultures. It is encouraging that some chaplains and parish or pastoral assistants have enrolled in transcultural nursing classes or are taking courses in anthropology. Likewise, community health and primary care nurses are also enrolling in courses to deal with culture care of their clients.

Although there are claims of a new health care reform, the author contends that any new reform must include transcultural health care and include the spiritual or religious needs of clients. Otherwise, the health system will fail, and only partial, fragmented and incomplete care will be offered. A related challenge is how best one can incorporate the spiritual dimensions with diverse care expectations. If grounded from a comparative cultural viewpoint, nurses have the opportunity to try different approaches to provide spiritual care to clients. For the ultimate potential for client recovery, to remain well or to die within a spiritual and religious context remains a major challenge to nurses and others in human services.

Unquestionably, nurses with a comparative spiritual and religious knowledge and competence can be extremely beneficial to clients. During life's most stressful moments, the nurse can give spiritual care to attain and maintain well-being and health or to help clients deal with grief, losses and dying. Spiritual caring can have a calming and consoling influence on the client. It can help the client and family members face death with hope and in a peaceful way. Remaining and praying with the client in a crises or death situation can bring comfort and solace to those involved. Spiritual caring often means spending time with the client, listening to and offering appropriate guidance that is congruent with the client's religious and spiritual needs. Bringing forth the spiritual caring dimensions to the client is often a great source of comfort and support, especially in times of tragedy or with news about a fatal disease or human condition. The use of transcultural spiritual-care constructs such as comfort, presence, support, understanding, listening, praying with, and giving hope and protection are a few of the many care expressions found in nurse-client relationships. The care constructs, however, are culturally based and are closely linked to the client's religious and spiritual beliefs. Culture-specific care can be highly beneficial.

Today, nurse-educators, researchers and clinicians are being challenged by consumers of different cultures to make their work culturally congruent to those they serve. With the use of the culture care theory, ethnonursing, and the new paradigm of transcultural caring, the nursing profession has great potential to transform nursing into quality-based caring, and to provide meaningful spiritual care to clients. Much more research, education and creative thinking in the day-to-day application of spiritual and religious care is needed, for spiritual caring can give nurses guidance in their decisions and in ways to serve clients in humane, sensitive, and compassionate ways.

In sum, we are living in a world that is rapidly changing, with refugees and people coming and going from many different places in the world. These people expect that nurses will fulfill and respect their spiritual and religious needs in a professional and skilled manner. Nurses, health personnel and religious leaders are challenged today to know and respond to diverse cultural groups in ways little known in the past. While war and economic and political factors have played a major part in our global multicultural movement, it has often been the religious and spiritual dimensions that have sustained newcomers and given them strength to face new and difficult life changes. Spiritual caring can give hope, patience, purpose in being and living, consolation, and often protection in cultural change movements. Nurses and health care providers of tomorrow will continue to discover the tremendous importance of spiritual care for the health and well-being of clients.

REFERENCES

Andrews M. and Boyle, J. (1995). *Transcultural Concepts in Nursing Care* (Second Edition). Philadelphia: J. P. Lippincott.

Barnum, B. (1995). *Spirituality in Nursing: Everything Old is New Again.* Nursing Leadership Forum (Vol. 1., pp. 24–30). New York: Springer Publishing Co.

Carson, V. B. (1989). *Spiritual Dimensions of Nursing Practice.* Philadelphia: W.B. Saunders.

Dobson, S. (1991). *Transcultural Nursing: A Contemporary Imperative.* London: Scutari Press.

Geertz, C. (1973). *The Interpretation of Cultures.* New York: Basic Books.

Hall, C. and Hilreth, L. (1993). "Spiritual caring behaviors as reported by Christian nurses." *Western Journal of Nursing Research, 15* (6), pp. 730–41.

Haviland, W. (1993). *Cultural Anthropology* (7th Ed.). Orlando: Harcourt, Brace, Jovanovich College Publisher.

Horn, B. (1990). "Cultural concepts and post partal care." *Journal of Transcultural Nursing, 2* (1), pp. 48–51.

——. (1995). "Transcultural nursing and child-rearing of the Muckleshoots." In M. Leininger (Ed.), *Transcultural Nursing: Concepts, Theories, Research, and Practices* (2nd ed.), pp. 501–14. New York: McGraw Hill Custom College Series.

Hsu, F. (1981). *Americans and Chinese: Passage to Differences.* Honolulu: University of Hawaii Press.

Kottak, C.P. (1991). *Anthropology: The Exploration of Human Diversity.* New York: McGraw Hill, Inc.

Lane, J. A. (1987). "The care of the human spirit." *Journal of Professional Nursing, 3*, pp. 332–37.

Leininger, M. (1970). *Nursing and Anthropology: Two Worlds to Blend.* New York: John Wiley and Sons.

——. (1974). "Humanism health and cultural values." In M. Leininger (Ed.), *Health Care Issues*, pp. 37–60. Philadelphia: F. A. Davis.

——. (1977). "The phenomena of caring: Caring as the essence and central focus of nursing." *American Nurses Foundation: Nursing Research Report, 12* (1), pp. 2–14.

——. (1978). *Transcultural Nursing: Theories, Concepts, and Practices.* New York: John Wiley and Sons.

——. (1981). *Care: An Essential Human Need.* Thorofare, N.J.: C. Slack and Co.

——. (1986). "Care facilitation and resistance factors in the culture of nursing." In. Z. Wolf (Ed.), *Clinical Care in Nursing.* Maryland: Associated Press.

——. (1990a). *Ethical and Moral Dimensions of Care.* Detroit: Wayne State University Press.

——. (1990b). "Spiritual Dimensions of Health: Transcultural Perspectives." Unpublished paper. University of Windsor, Canada.

——. (1993). "Gadsup of Papua New Guinea revisited: A three decades view." *Journal of Transcultural Nursing, 5* (1), pp. 21–30.

——. (1995). *Transcultural Nursing: Concepts, Theories, Research, and Practices* (Second Edition). New York: McGraw-Hill Custom College Series.

——. (Ed.) (1988). *Care: The Essence of Nursing and Health.* Detroit: Wayne State University Press (originally published by Slack, 1984).

——. (Ed.). (1991). *Culture care diversity and universality: A theory of nursing.* New York: National League for Nursing.

Longway, I. (1970). "Toward a philosophy of nursing." *Journal of Adventist Education, 32* (3), pp. 20–27.

Major, J. S. (1989). *The Land and People of China.* New York: J. P. Lippincott.

Mashiba, G. (1995). "Culturally based health - illness patterns in South Africa and humanistic nursing care practices." In M. Leininger (Ed.)

McFarland (1994). *Cultural Care of Anglo- and African American Elderly Resident within the Environmental Context of a Long-term Care Institution.* Dissertation. Unpublished manuscript. Detroit: Wayne State University, College of Nursing.

Merriam-Webster, Incorporated (1994). Springfield, MA.

Oswalt, W. (1986). *Life Cycles and Lifeways: An Introduction to Cultural Anthropology.* Palo Alto: Mayfield Publishing Co.

Phillips, S. and Lobar, S. (1995). "Navajo child health beliefs and rearing practices within a transcultural nursing framework: Literature review." In M. Leininger (Ed.), *Transcultural Nursing: Concepts, Theories, Research, and Practices* (Second Edition), pp. 485–500. New York: McGraw-Hill Custom College Series.

Quinn, J. F. (1992). "Holding sacred space: The nurse as healing environment." *Holistic Nursing Practice, 6* (4), pp. 26–36.

Ray, M. (1989). "Transcultural caring: Political and economic vision." *Journal of Transcultural Nursing, 1* (1), pp. 17–21.

Roach, S. (1992). *The human act of caring: A blueprint for the health professions* (Rev. ed.). Ottawa: Canadian Hospital Association Press.

Rosenbaum, J. N. (1990). *Cultural care, cultural health, and grief phenomena related to older Greek-Canadian widows within Leininger's theory of culture care*. Unpublished manuscript. Wayne State University, College of Nursing, Detroit.

Stasiak (1991). "Culture care theory with Mexican Americans in an urban context." In M. Leininger (Ed.), *Culture Care Diversity and Universality: A Theory of Nursing*. New York: National League for Nursing Press.

Watson, J. (1985). *Nursing: Human Science and Human Care: A Theory of Nursing*. Norwalk, Conn.: Appleton Century Crofts.

Wenger, A. F. Z. (1988). The phenomenon of care in a high context culture: The Old Order Amish. (Doctoral dissertation, Wayne State University, 1988/1989). *Dissertation Abstracts International, 50–02B*, 500.

Williams, T. (1990). *Cultural Anthropology*. Englewood Cliffs, N.J.: Prentice Hall.

The Spirituality of Caring: Transformation to a Participatory Consciousness

M. Patrice McCarthy

Introduction

Even a cursory glance at newspaper or news magazine headlines turns one's attention to the societal discord present at both the local and global levels. Whether a report of outright civil war, domestic violence or assessment of the desensitization of youth to violence the reports give credence to a growing sense of anxiety about the demise of civilized society. The perceived regression of social mores supports skepticism, an urge toward protective isolationism and a lack of hope about the future. It is in this context that the issue of caring and its spiritual foundations emerges as a central concern in postmodern society. Rather than unrealistic rhetoric explication of the spiritual roots of caring provides a foundation for understanding an ethic of care in its full moral and political contexts. As a foundation for a consciousness supportive of a peaceful society, caring is a practice that offers hope for the future (Tronto, 1993).

The work of philosopher Beatrice Bruteau provides a substantive explanation for an understanding of the social relevance of caring in the larger context of communal relations. It is Bruteau's (1977, 1985) premise that the current social consciousness is derived from a hierarchical valuing system. This orientation sustains a mentality that inappropriately assigns value by a system of contrast of one object, one person, one race or one gender over another. As an evaluative system, it establishes identity by contrast and mutual negation. Within this system, a person is valued by possession of specific traits or qualities. The assignment of value to individuals, races or a class of people based on the possession of particular traits on what one *has* rather than on who one *is,* sustains a genealogy of injustice (Bruteau, 1977). In Bruteau's words, "When real persons are valued according to an abstraction scale, (it) precipitates emotions associated with the domination paradigm and behavior follows the emotions.... As long as we persist in this basic perception of *people as alienated from one another, valued and judged in terms of various abstract qualities,* ranked according to who dominates whom, so long will it be psychologically impossible for us to desist from the practice of injustice. What has to change is the primary perception of being itself. We have to break with the identification system based on abstractions and liberate ourselves to perceive persons in their concrete wholeness" (Bruteau, 1977, p.177).

The Foundation of a Participatory Consciousness

The development of the social consciousness that Bruteau refers to is premised on a transformation of values. The foundation of a participatory consciousness is based on an understanding of the person as a whole, differentiated being whose value is inherent in one's existence as a spiritual being. It is a progression beyond the categorizing of abstract qualities. The nature of this social consciousness operates on the basis of intellectual intuition or insight that is act of the spirit. As an act of the spirit, each individual is appreciated for his or her unique wholeness. The insight that is possible from this vantage point is derived as an act of cognition that is simultaneously an act of spiritual sympathy. The nature of this social consciousness recognizes the ultimate unity of all of nature and the concrete wholeness and preciousness of each individual that comprise the whole. Rather than individuals seen as merely parts of a new whole, each individual is seen as a whole, concrete being each valued equally.

The nature of person in this participatory, relational perspective is defined by self-giving, as love enacted as caring (1984). In this context, persons come to know themselves and others in the process of life lived moment-to-moment and self-to-other. By moving to the spiritual foundation as a means for defining "person," the psychological level of ego and the reactive, protective actions that appropriately operate at the level of ego are integrated into a fuller appreciation of oneself and of others. The self-giving of the person is based on an act of creative freedom that arises from the spirit (Bruteau, 1983). This creative freedom is distinctly different from the choice freedom of the psychological level. Choice freedom is a selection of alternatives posed by the environment. While the act is "free," it does not originate purely from within, but rather is a reaction to an externally posed option. Creative freedom is called "creative" because "it arises out of nothing, not having any predecessor" (Bruteau, 1987, p. 202).

The participatory consciousness shifts the center of life and living to the present. As life is an act of the spirit lived in the present moment, the memory of who an individual was in the past is secondary to where and how he or she is now in life. The process of life lived in the present moment shifts attention away from the psychological level of action/reaction that is characterized by choice freedom. The shift to the spiritual life transcends the level of descriptions and the psychological level to the energy of the spiritual will, to where that person is now in his or her own process of creating life. The intent of the spiritual will is to contribute to the creation of another person in a mutually affirming process. As a personal act, self-giving is based on an integration of knowing, willing, imagining and feeling. It is in this process that the future is created freely; the act of life, of self-giving, is an act of creating the future.

The creation of the future is supported as persons join in an appreciation of one another where they are in their lives—a cycle described as one of enstasy and ecstasy (Bruteau, 1977). The cycle is two aspects of response each participant experiences in a relationship. Ecstasy is a posture adopted by one person toward another that allows that person to experience what the other person is experiencing as the person experiences it. This results in a true level of intimacy where experiences are shared by both parties in a relationship. The other dimension of this cycle is enstasy. Enstasy exists when one individual is aware of his/her own experience, an awareness that is a knowledge of oneself. Enstasy is a kind of self-reflection, a realization that is a revelation about one's life that results in the reach for new horizons and deeper awareness of oneself as a person.

The final dimension of a participatory consciousness rests in the act of two persons reaching beyond themselves, extending their love as a dyad toward yet a third person where that person is in his or her life process. The most profound example of action by an ecstatic couple, as described above, is a couple joining to bring a new life into being. In its most profound and ideal sense, the joy and ecstasy of the physical and spiritual union of sexual intercourse exemplifies the building of community by extending love toward yet another person. The critical distinction of this relational foundation rests in the clarity of boundaries that allows for each person to be in his or her own life process while sharing life with others. In this process, life is based on intellectual insight that is an act of the spirit, through unconditional love toward another. Each individual acts as a whole, differentiated being that shares life and builds the future by mutually affirming the existence of another.

An example from the everyday world of human experience that depicts the type of relationships described above can be found in the fellowship of Alcoholics Anonymous (AA). The fundamental premise of relationship in this group process is the movement of the Spirit as the means for healing that emerges in the recovery process. Each individual is acknowledged and loved for where he/she is in the recovery process. The hallmark of this dynamic is that each person is supported in the discovery of his/her true self unknown to him or her and to others as a result of alcoholism. There is a mutual recognition of others as having shared a life experience, regardless of the specific facts or "qualifying" events. What is recognized in others encountered in the recovery process is the loss of self that occurred in the alcoholic process. This loss of self constitutes a total separation of self from the world: physical, spiritual, emotional and mental. The support of one another that occurs through relationships formed in AA is premised on a faith in the Spirit that moves among them.

Caring From the Heart

The spiritual origins of caring give definition to new moral boundaries and pave the way for an inclusive view of the world. This relational world view derives its meaning from an appreciation of the unique contribution of men and women from different cultures, races and backgrounds. From this vantage point, the focus shifts to understanding the person as a spiritual, transcendent and relational being (McCarthy, 1992). In this context the person is understood as inherently a being-in-community who experiences and contributes to definition of both self and one's community in a contemporaneous manner. This personal and communal dynamic provides a new perspective from which one can view life's experiences and one's contribution to communal development.

PROGRESSING BEYOND THE EGO: THE ROLE OF TRANSCENDENCE AS PROCESS

The notion of transcendence is generally reserved as a descriptor of God. It is in this sense that an understanding of the term would seem not to apply to human capabilities. But in the context of understanding the relevance of the term as it is applied to the person, it is critical to understand the nature of what is meant by transcendence as a process of a spiritual life.

Over the history of western society, the term "transcendence" has had multiple meanings and referents (Underhill, 1990). In common parlance, transcendence has been understood as the seeking of that which is separate from and beyond the human being. The relevance of the term to understanding the process and experience of spirituality requires clarity in an understanding of the term. The process of transcendence is inherent to human existence. It is an outgrowth of the basic anxiety that exists because we know, as human beings, that we are not yet what we long to be; "We are interminably in the painful process of self-transcendence toward fullness of being" (Frohlich, 1994). It is this awareness that describes the gap between who we are at a given moment and the wholeness that we long for. This gap is the awareness of a desire for greater self-discovery and self-knowledge. It is also in this process that the potential for healing and growth occurs.

Bernard Lonergan (1957), a preeminent twentieth-century philosopher and theologian, identified the source of transcendence as human beings' insatiable desire to know that continuously seeks to go beyond one's present knowledge. Transcendence, then, is not the search for something separate, distant or beyond the individual. But rather, it is that which "picks up, corrects and extends the horizons of human nature" (Williams, 1988, p.339). It is a going further in our understanding of ourselves without separating from prior insights. Rather than an ascent away from that which is transcended, it is a movement toward it, recaptured, intensified and transfigured (Levy-Bruel, 1966). In this sense, prior impressions are reinterpreted and integrated into a more informed understanding of one's self. Wilber (1990) describes the process of transcendence as one of integration that includes all understandings held throughout the process of change and growth to new horizons. The process of transcendence extends and involves the fullness of the person: mentally, physically and spiritually.

The experience of transcendence is an awakening of new insight, new understanding and new self-knowledge. In the progression beyond the psychological level of ego function that Bruteau delineates as the way of the spiritual life, the spiritual life becomes a discovery not only of one's own enhanced sense of being but a greater appreciation for the sense of where others are in understanding their own lives. The nature of human knowing extends well beyond the rational; it involves experience, understanding and judgement; none of these three alone or in combination of two of the three represent the totality of human knowing (Lonergan, 1988).

The fullness of human knowing is informed by seeing, hearing, inquiring, imagining, understanding, conceiving. It is the fullness of experience, with an understanding coupled with a judgement that is the dynamic structure of human existence. "The dynamic structure of human knowing intends being. That intention...is the originating drive of human knowing. Consciously, intelligently, rationally it goes beyond data to intelligibility; beyond intelligibility to truth and through truth to being; and beyond truth and being to the truth and being still to know. But though it goes beyond, it does not leave behind. It goes beyond to add and, when it has added, it unites" (Lonergan, 1988, p. 230).

The experience of this process of discovery has been described by Kurtz and Ketcham (1992) as a spirituality of imperfection. In this sense, it is the recognition of the "not yet fully who we may become" that is acknowledged as the imperfect nature of what it means to be human. It is in the paradox of the desire for wholeness and the awareness of human imperfection that one discovers spirituality. This awareness speaks to both the "inevitability of pain and the possibility of healing within the pain" (p.3). The search for the understanding of one's human limitations allows an easing of one's pain as well as an understanding of what it means to hurt and what it means to heal. It begins with the recognition that trying to be perfect is the most tragic of human mistakes. When life flows from the insight that trying to "play God" is fraught with problems, one is able to accept the inability to control every aspect of one's life. The consequence of this awareness is the peace and serenity that the pretense of power, money, possessions, privilege, drugs or alcohol "promise but never deliver" (p.5).

The process of discovering the intellectual insight at the root of the spiritual perspective provides a foundation that fosters integration of the physical, the emotional and the intellectual in a grounded holistic framework. The process of consciousness raising is an example of how discovery of diverse feelings gives way to discernment and understanding (Griffiths, 1988). In this process, feelings perceived as uniquely personal and disconnected from rational thought are brought to mind for reflection. These feelings serve as a basis for discussion with others and are used as an instrument to expand understanding. The expanded understanding involves subjective experience as well as a means for expanding insight and knowledge about the emotional, physical, political and social dimensions of experience. As a consequence of this process, connections are made between previously disconnected thoughts and feelings. Feelings, rather than being disconnected from rational thought, are put in the service of an expanding awareness and knowledge of specifically personal situations. In addition, the universal qualities of situations are discovered during dialogue with others. Feelings are then linked with thoughts and boundaries are established around that which is personal and that which is shared with others. In this process, experience becomes integrated on a personal level and also recognized as a common ground for a shared humanity and thus becomes an opportunity for building community.

As an example of transcendence, the work of discernment inherent to consciousness raising extends the bounds of how one perceives self and others. This process is an example of what Buber (1970) defines as the process of engaging in the world that involves the whole person. It expands the depth of one's insight by integrating all of the human activities: thinking, feeling, wishing, hoping, reflecting and responding. In this mode of experiencing the world, one turns toward the world and becomes engaged in a dialogue of openness and awareness that transforms the world. The transformation is from a view of the world as an object to be used for one's pleasure and purpose to a view of those we encounter as a subject with an interiority that is shared in community. This mode of awareness can be characterized as a "becoming aware" that is in contrast to an "observing" posture. An observing posture looks upon others as objects separate from oneself, while a posture of becoming aware orients us to view others as addressing something to us. It is this posture that entails the intent of establishing a relation, a dialogue that begins with an attitude of attention to others as whole persons.

PERSON AS A RELATIONAL BEING

Psychological theories describe a progression of maturity as a series of stages from infancy to adulthood marked by degrees of dependence and independence. The term "interdependence" is the descriptor of maturity that acknowledges the role that others play in the cooperative endeavors of society. While appropriate as descriptors of psychological growth and social function, these terms are actually an incomplete representation of the potential of the human being as a spiritual person. It is the love that flows from the person as "freely projected energy" that enables a progression to a view of the person as an inter-independent being (Bruteau, 1985). Interdependence is based on scarcity and deprivation. It arises out of a perception of others possessing something that we need and vice versa.

An interindependent being understands "sharing not as a need imposed by scarcity but as a value in itself" that arises out of the superabundance of love. Caring from the heart flows out of a sense of confidence in one's self as a distinct being, but one who also acknowledges how one's response to others can influence their lives, decisions and processes. In this sense, caring is not a "doing for" but rather a "presence with" them in their efforts to understand themselves in their own lives. This empathic posture adopted toward others is exemplified by the support extended during those life experiences that require learning new insights about oneself in relation to others. The reaching out to others is based on a shared experience that creates life. The nature of this relationship creates community out of a superabundance of love that flows from the heart. The protective nature of the psychological level functions from a posture of deficiency. By necessity, the ego must protect its boundaries from the intrusion of others, appropriately so for this level of function. But the personal energy of the spiritual life is liberated in the interest of creating life rather than protecting the ego. While "this attitude does not mean that the earth will not run short of oil or clean water; it does, however, imply that we can deal with such problems more freely and creatively than is possible given our present mentality" (Bruteau, 1985, p. 203).

COMMUNITY AS A SHARED SPIRITUAL JOURNEY

When we embark on any journey, we set off in a direction of our choosing and, likely as not, get detoured because of weather problems, late planes and lost luggage. And as on any trip of unknown duration we take along baggage for the trip. We take some of our favorite clothes, things we hate to leave behind and those things we think we can't do without. And likely as not we take along too much.

A spiritual journey is not unlike the journey I just described. We live our lives sometimes in the directions of our choosing. We take along the baggage that we think is essential to our identities. Baggage in this case is in the form of our pride, our egos, our cultural heritage and maybe our sense of independence. Just like our other journey, we encounter situations that detour us, often not of our choosing, but ones which present challenges that enable us to continue on. A unique dimension of a spiritual journey though, is that it is the baggage that we brought with us that we need to lose. It is the nature of the spiritual journey to present us with experiences that confound our abilities to proceed. We are faced with a paradox that defies our abilities to proceed in the same way as before. We must lose the baggage of our pride, our egos, and our self-centeredness. What we must lose is the baggage that binds us to our old ways of being, our old ways of thinking and most importantly, our old ways of interacting with those people with whom we share the world.

Regardless of whether we speak about a spiritual journey from a Judeo-Christian, Buddhist, Sufi, Islamic, Hindu or Taoist tradition the spiritual journey is "an awakening awareness and conscious attunement to the sacred source of life" (Mische, 1982). Spirituality is quite distinct from religion and religious dogma. It is a search for meaning in life, the process of ordering life in intimate communion with this sacred center. We may address the sacred source as God, Yahweh, Jesus, Allah or Buddha. The name will flow from each person's specific spiritual orientation. What is critical is that each individual, each culture, has defined a way of depicting that which enables one's own search for discovery of the mystery of life and the search for that which sustains one on the path of life. A universal characteristic of the spiritual journey is confrontation with the limitations of being human, with all our imperfections, uncertainties and our mortality. It is also a process of discovery through the experience of the paradox.

A paradox can best be described as an impasse: a feeling of no way out, no way around, no rational escape, no possibilities in a situation, a situation where every logical solution remains unsatisfying at the least. There is an experience of powerlessness and a lack of assurance of those support systems one is accustomed to relying on. There is also another dimension of impasse that has been discussed by philosophers, poets, psychologists, theologians and mystics. The historical theologian Belden Lane (1981) describes it like this, "...in a genuine impasse one's accustomed way of acting and living is brought to a standstill. The left side of the brain, with its usual application of linear, conventional thinking is ground to a halt. The impasse forces us to start all over again, driving us to contemplation. On the other hand, the impasse provides a challenge and a concrete focus for contemplation.... It forces the right side of the brain into gear, seeking intuitive, symbolic, unconventional answers, so that action can be renewed eventually with greater purpose" (Lane, 1981, p. 200). The paradox is a situation perceived as one without potential that is actually loaded with potential. Impasse becomes the place for reconstitution of the intuitive self. A genuine impasse situation is such that the more action one applies to escape it, the worse it gets. It is when the powerlessness of the impasse becomes the focus for reflection that the resolution of the paradox comes from the unexpected, the new vision. The impasse of the spiritual journey can be an opportunity for creative growth and transformation if the experience of the impasse is fully incorporated into one's heart with consciousness and consent, if the limitations of one's humanity and the human condition are squarely faced and experienced as an existential powerlessness, and if the ego does not demand understanding in the name of control and predictability but is willing to submit to the mystery and the unknown. We can identify paradoxical situations at the personal, professional and global levels.

In our personal lives we experience a paradox when we are the victims of repeated physical abuse in societies that offer little or no awareness of the destruction to human life perpetuated by a lack of intervention. We experience the paradox of the spiritual journey when we continue to give birth to children, only to experience the heartache of watching them go off to war.

In our community as nurse and health care providers, we live in a world of paradox. We all experience attempting to provide care to those who live in such overwhelming stress that any action seems like a thumb in the hole of a dam. In the United States we experience repeated frustration in our inability to provide care that is needed because others have defined what constitutes appropriate care and what will be paid for. In South America nurses attempt to provide health care and social services in countries ravaged by war and the resulting national instability that consumes the energies of the people and the natural resources of the countries. Throughout the world there is a struggle for dollars to support programs capable of improving the health and welfare of the people, only to have programs of a more technical nature seen as more important.

In the international community we have the staple food resources to feed an additional 1.5 billion people. Yet there is widespread famine on many continents of the world. There is virtually no continent untouched by the increasing percentages of people who are not able to get enough to eat. In addition to worldwide hunger, there are global problems of pollution, unemployment, inflation and genocide in the wake of centuries-old hatred. In the face of the magnitude of these problems, we experience a despair and fear for the fragility of a peaceful world future.

Each of these examples is representative of the same process. Each can be viewed as an impasse on the individual or communal level that requires a new way of thinking, a new way of organizing that is cooperative, not competitive. There is a flow between the collective earth journey and our personal journeys. They cannot be separated. We are all in the process of becoming. The earth is in a dynamic process of becoming, and so are all of its inhabitants—the trees, plants and flowers. Humans are all a part of a developing world that is a part of a larger developing world community. In a certain sense, we make our journey alone; no one can make it for us. But in another sense we make the journey together. The authentic spiritual journey can never be an escape from life's problems. As individuals and as a global community we are all called to respond to the need for creative response to the global crisis of today. Engagement in a conscious way with the spiritual journey is not just a problem-solving process, although it ultimately leads to that. It leads to a spiritual transformation that is essential for moving beyond the reality of the paradox we face.

But moving beyond the paradox, the impasse, is a difficult process. Perhaps the best image of the spiritual journey is the spiral; the spiral travels inward, outward and forward. All these directions are a part of a flow; a flow that develops in inner relationship to transcendental reality; in outward relationship to the human community and the whole earth community; and forward as relationships to future generations require conscious participation in creating a future that offers hope. The inner journey is a journey to the sacred source at the center of every being and all being. On the inner journey we confront our deepest past and all that formed it. In the words of Patricia Mische (1985), "We are standing at the gateway to outer space and the gateway to our inner space, and we are at the point of discovering that they are the same space. The inner space and the outer space are one space. It is holy space. It is the space of divine activity" (p. 123).

At the nucleus of the journey, we discover the place where, having confessed our participation in the world's sin history, we discover our participation in the world's grace history—in the Buddha nature, the Christ nature, the Tao. It is where we discover that we are sacred beings.

The outward dimension of the spiritual journey seeks to discover the gifts and wisdom of the cultures of the earth. It recognizes the strength and wisdom of Hinduism, Buddhism, Islam, Judaism, Christianity and the tribal religions. It also seeks to discover the wisdom of the goddess traditions lost to a world consumed by patriarchal definitions of the deity depicted exclusively as male.

The forward journey is a journey of a new genesis. Thomas Berry (1979) describes the world order as a "product of the world process. In its human phase, world order is a continuation of the cosmic/earth process. The "order" involved is not the order of an abiding image of eternity such as that presented by Plato...but the order of a universe and a human community that is coming into being. This sense that the human order is a continuation and participation in an emerging world process is primary in our discussion. There is not, and never has been, an established world order. There is only the world genesis: a cosmogenesis, biogenesis, anthropogenesis" (p. 6).

I think the key to moving beyond the impasses we experience comes first with an engagement with our journey with a sense of humility—not with a sense of humility that is self-effacing, but with a modesty that acknowledges strength and imperfection, gifts and limitations. Humility enables us to step aside from the needs of our egos and the fear of our human imperfections. Humility enables us to accept our vulnerabilities and to seek forgiveness from those we have harmed. Humility enables the acceptance of our individual gifts, those we received from our heritage and those which are the unique expression of our presence in the world. These gifts may come in the form of patient companion, negotiator, strength of conviction. Acceptance of one's own gifts prepares one to accept the gifts of others. Most importantly, a spiritual transformation makes us aware that we are not alone in life, that we are coparticipants with the universe that is evolving with us.

Movement beyond the paradox frees us from the structures that bind us to the fears of our differences and from mental structures that enable us to perpetuate dominance over others based on a need to control. Discovery of the inner core of our worth enables us to ask new questions and find a source of renewal in the face of frustration and potential despair. In our personal lives, we can discover new ways of being with and accepting ourselves. We can ask ourselves what gifts we have to offer the world and believe that there is an answer. In our health care community, we seek to discover from those we serve what sustains and nurtures. In our world we can face the challenge of removing structures that contribute to the exploitation of the peoples and resources of the earth for the benefit of a few.

When we have a sense of our own gifts and the gifts of others, we are able to see our mutuality with the peoples of the world and with the natural world. When this happens we are propelled into making connections that were unseen before. In the words of Patricia Mische, "We must be far-sighted enough to plant seeds now toward a new genesis so that our descendants will look back on us as ancestors who brought honor and life to them and the planetary community...that while the whole responsibility for the future of the world does not rest on any one person's shoulders, we each have a unique task to do in forwarding a more human world order" (p.6).

Acknowledging the spiritual foundation of caring reestablishes the integrity of a life process trivialized by marketing strategies that use it to boost the sales of material commodities. The profound is often found in the simple. This is the case when one considers a principle like that found in the caring process. But the renewal of appreciation for the consequences of truly caring from the heart is a staggering reality to consider. One must be in awe of its magnitude and its mystery. The benefits of the technological age that dominated the twentieth century have made contact among human beings immediately possible. But the challenge of the twenty-first century is to learn to live with one another, to understand the commonality of the human condition, to address one another from a posture of compassion and mutual affirmation, and become co-participants in life's energies and creators of world peace through love, compassion and justice. It is in this sense that the challenges of the future hold promise designed with integrity and respect for those who will come after us.

REFERENCES

Berry, T. (1979). The ecological age. *The Whole Earth Papers*, No. 12. East Orange, New Jersey: Global Education Associates.

Bruteau, B. (1977). Neo-feminism and the next revolution in consciousness. *Cross Currents,* 27(2), 170–82.

——. (1983). The living one: Transcendent freedom creates the future. *Cistercian Studies,* 18(1), 42–58.

——. (1984). Activating human energy for the grand option. *Cistercian Studies,* 19(2), 151–62.

——. (1985). Global spirituality and the integration of the east and west. *Cross Currents,* 35(2), 190–205.

——. (1987). Trinitarian personhood. *Cistercian Studies,* 22(3), 199–212.

Buber, M. (1970). *I and thou.* (Trans. W. Kaufmann). New York: Charles Scribner's Sons.

Frohlich, M. (1994). From mystification to mystery: Lonergan and the theological significance of sexuality. In C. Crysdale (Ed.),

Lonergan and feminism (pp.175–98). Toronto: University of Toronto Press.

Griffiths, M. (1988). Feminism, feelings and philosophy. In M. Griffiths and M. Whitford (Eds.), *Feminist perspectives in philosophy* (pp. 131–51). Bloomington: Indiana University Press.

Kurtz, E. and Ketcham, K. (1992). *The spirituality of imperfection.* New York: Bantam Books.

Lane, B. C. (1981). Spirituality and political commitment: Notes on a liberation theology of nonviolence. *America,* 144, 197–202.

Levy-Bruel, L. (1966). *How natives think.* New York: Washington Square Press. Originally published in 1910 as *Les fonctions mentales dans societas inferieures.*

Lonergan, B. J. F. (1957). *Insight: A study of human understanding.* San Francisco: Harper and Row, Publishers.

——. (1988). Cognitional structure. In F. E. Crowe and R. M. Doran (Eds.), *Collection* (2nd ed.). (pp. 230–42). Toronto: University Press.

McCarthy, M. P. (1992). *A relational ontology: The interplay of transcendence, spirituality and community.* Unpublished doctoral dissertation, University of Colorado, Denver.

Mische, P. (1982). Toward a global spirituality. *The Whole Earth Papers,* No. 16. New York: Global Education Associates.

——. (1985). *Star Wars and the state of our souls.* Minneapolis: Winston Press, Inc.

Tronto, J. C. (1993). *Moral boundaries: A political argument for an ethic of care.* London: Routledge, Chapman, and Hall, Inc.

Underhill, E. (1990). *Mysticism.* New York: Image Books, Doubleday.

Wilber, K. (1990). *Eye to eye: The quest for the new paradigm.* Boston: Shambhala.

Williams, G.B. (1988). Transcendence and the development of consciousness. *Studies in Formative Spirituality: The Journal of Ongoing Formation, 9* (3), 339–54.

How Spirituality Transforms the Care of Older Persons

Cheryl A. McCulloch

Case Study

The following case is presented as a way to ground the discussion of this paper in the everyday discourse of practice and to outline how spirituality transforms caring for older persons:

Lillian, a seventy-five-year-old married woman with end-stage Parkinson's disease, sepsis, pressure ulcers, depression and dementia was admitted to the hospital from a nursing home. Withdrawn and showing signs of regression, she would lay in the fetal position and offer only limited responses, frequently echoing, "carry me out in a black box." Husband Jim was a strong advocate and visited daily. Two grown sons and their families were less involved. As a clinical nurse specialist, I became involved with Lillian's case through the need for expert consultation regarding the care for her pressure ulcers. Each day I visited, she did not open her eyes or respond in any way. I would introduce myself each time and spend a few minutes with her, often holding her contracted fingers in mine. One day, after about two weeks, as I was talking with Lillian, she opened her eyes and looked directly at me. When I asked Lillian what we could do for her, she requested to see a minister. Near the end of that visit, Lillian asked to pray the Lord's Prayer. Gradually Lillian started to respond to those around her, developing strong caring relationships with staff and the minister that visited weekly. It became evident that she was not suffering from dementia and was in fact as sharp as a tack mentally. Eventually, through hard work, perseverance and humour, Lillian regained the ability to feed herself, walk with a walker and to be continent. Her sacral pressure ulcer healed completely. She was also able to make weekly visits to her home with her husband. The strength to endure, respond and hope came from the caring relationships that Lillian experienced around her. Recognizing her uniqueness as a person, as well as the relentless drive to reach across the abyss of her unresponsiveness, were key components within the caring relationship that resulted in rekindling the fire of her spirit.

Introduction

Humanistic caring for institutionalized older persons in western society remains a formidable challenge. Ageism, coupled with economic constraints and ethical concerns, such as euthanasia, are major factors influencing the nature of our caring ethic. Despite holistic ideals, caring in institutional settings still remains primarily focused on meeting the physical needs of older persons. Dignity and respect for older persons as individuals are frequently neglected or entirely overlooked. The purpose of this chapter is to explore how spirituality transforms caring for older persons. By refocusing caring to incorporate the spirituality of older persons, a number of important outcomes may be achieved. First, personhood of older individuals may be acknowledged and reaffirmed. Second, quality of life may be positively influenced for institutionalized older people. Third, humanistic caring from the heart may be rediscovered by care providers. And finally, caring for older persons may be revitalized within our institutions and society.

Aging and Spirituality

The spiritual dimensions of aging are deemed to be more important than the biological changes (Bianchi, 1982). Yet, the biological changes usually attract the most attention from health care providers. Aging presents many unique spiritual challenges for older persons (Berggren-Thomas and Griggs, 1995). Chronic illness and functional decline can distort an older person's sense of personhood and impact on the potentials for spiritual growth in both positive and negative ways. Dependency on others is one of the most important negative predictors of older persons' perceptions of quality of life (Barron McBride, 1993). Furthermore, the loss of functional abilities such as mobility, toiletting and feeding are strong predictors of the need for institutional care. Making the transition to living in a long-term-care facility is extremely stressful and even life threatening for some older people. A high number of the elderly die within the first year of living in a long- term-care facility (Bohuslawsky, 1989). Older persons have a strong need to find meaning in aging and answers to why they are losing their independence, dignity and capacities. Spirituality can provide a means for older persons to find meaning and purpose in life despite disabilities.

Other significant losses such as retirement and the death of loved ones bring about changes in relationships and social networks. These losses can alter an older individual's sense of self (Bianchi, 1982). Western society values productivity and material wealth as a measure of personal worth. This belief can become a self-fulfilling prophecy for older persons (Hirst and Metcalf, 1984). Erickson (1968) describes the major developmental task of late-life as ego integrity versus despair. For example, retired persons achieve integrity when they seek other means of productivity to satisfy their needs. Focusing on the spirituality of older persons may provide a means to help individuals through these difficult adjustments and late-life developmental tasks.

Cherished beliefs and values developed throughout life are part of an older person's spirituality. They act as a guiding force through troubled waters. Shrinking social networks and the loss of loved ones means that the aged often have an acute need for human touch, love and relatedness. Spirituality provides a way for older persons to cope with life changes through the unconditional love of a higher being or another person. Pieper (1981) identifies social interaction, emotional support and enhancing spiritual growth as the benefits that older persons derive from church attendance. A positive relationship between self-esteem and the degree of religious orientation is also identified in older persons (Nelson, 1990).

Studies demonstrate that spirituality takes on new dimensions and meaning for the aged and terminally ill who may be confronting death (Reed, 1987). Spirituality provides a means for forgiveness and hope for the future. Persons with strong religious convictions have been found to fear death less than nonreligious persons (Brennan and Missine, 1980). The actual process of dying, however, may still be a threatening experience even for those with strong religious beliefs. Transcending life's transgressions and hardships is a major aspect of spirituality.

Viktor Frankl (1967), writing about the experiences of Jewish survivors of the holocaust, offers hope and spirituality as a means to transcend difficult experiences and derive a sense of purpose in life.

Human uniqueness means that the experience of spirituality varies according to life experiences, insight, values and beliefs. The way in which the spirit interacts with the mind and the body is a mystery. Labun (1988) uses the metaphor of ions to describe the interrelationship between the three elements of mind, body and spirit. Each ion, although unique, when combined with other ions, forms a new compound. In a similar way, the spiritual self in combination with the mind and body react to situations as a totality. In each experience, there is a new unfolding reality. Stress provides an example of how the mind, body and spirit are affected in totality during the experience of a myocardial infarction or heart attack. Physically, the person may experience chest pain and/or shortness of breath; the emotions of anxiety and fear may be triggered, which in turn may stimulate a questioning of the meaning or purpose of life. When only the physical symptoms are addressed, the other major dimensions of personhood, mind and spirit are neglected.

SPIRITUALITY AND CARING

Humanistic caring requires a holistic approach to the body, mind and spirit of the older person. There is, however, very little information about what is meant by the spirit or spirituality. Spirituality is often equated with organized religious traditions— Protestant, Catholic or Jewish (Peterson, 1985). More recently, however, spirituality has been defined as an inherent quality of all humans that is important to health and well-being (Haase, Britt, Coward, Leidy and Penn, 1992; Reed, 1992).

Spirituality is a complex, multifaceted phenomenon that is difficult to define specifically. Conceptual analyses have identified some of the key attributes and components of spirituality as: (a) harmonious interconnectedness to others, nature, the universe or God, (b) belief in something greater than self, (c) inner strength or energy which is dynamic and constantly in flux and, (d) unfolding mystery (Burkhardt, 1989; Haase et al., 1992; Hungelmann, Kenkel-Rossi, Klassen and Stollenwerk, 1985). When spirituality was compared with the similar concepts of hope, acceptance and self-transcendence, connectedness with others emerged as the central theme (Haase et al., 1992). Buber (1947) also emphasizes this relational aspect of spirituality by maintaining that spirituality does not exist within a person but rather between persons.

Burkhardt (1989) differentiates religion from spirituality by identifying religion as the adherence to a belief system, and spirituality as the actual experience or connection with a higher being (Burkhardt, 1989). Furthermore, Reed (1987) defines spirituality, "in terms of personal views and behaviours that express a sense of relatedness to a transcendent dimension or to something greater than the self (p.336)." The notions of transcendence and connectedness are also present in the work of other nurse-scholars (Lane, 1987; Peterson, 1985).

Spirituality can include a number of other dimensions such as love, faith, hope, trust, generativity, inner meaning, mystical experience and religious behaviors (Labun, 1988; Lane, 1987; Reed, 1992).

The lived experiences or outcomes associated with spirituality usually signal personal growth and development. Three such outcomes include: (1) a sense of purpose or meaning in life, (2) a set of values to guide one's conduct and, (3) a feeling of self-transcendence that implies reaching out and/or rising above personal concerns (Haase et al., 1992). Lane (1987) describes other outcomes associated with spirituality as: inward turning and reflection, surrender, commitment and struggle. Spirituality also provides a means of forgiveness and personal healing for the older person. A number of nursing theorists including Parse (1981), Rogers (1970), and Watson (1988), often include the dimension of spirituality through the concept of transcendence in their nursing theories. Despite this, however, caring approaches within nursing remain inadequate to understand, celebrate and support spiritual growth in older persons.

Caring and spirituality then, seem to be inextricably bound within the notion of connectedness. Caring is defined here, as the human mode of being in relationship with others (Roach, 1984; Noddings, 1984). Caring is influenced by the attributes of the involved parties, both care provider and older person. Caring varies in intensity and duration over time, and is expressed through concrete behaviors and caring processes. Caring is relational and may be characterized by receptivity, relatedness and responsiveness (Noddings, 1984). The ultimate goal of caring is to benefit others, and results in caring outcomes for all involved parties. Figure 1 displays these essential aspects of caring in a framework which has been developed as a nursing practice model at Scarborough Grace Hospital, Scarborough, Ontario, Canada. Through the use of this caring practice model, the health care provider and older person together within a caring relationship, can focus on spirituality by: (a) identifying the older person's specific caring attributes that may relate to spirituality, (b) selecting and engaging in caring processes that foster spiritual growth and, (c) travelling together on the older person's spiritual journey through the illness experience toward spiritual caring outcomes.

Spiritual transformation occurs when hopefulness and/or harmony are restored; when reconciliation or healing has occurred; when the older person can transcend present difficulties and focus on deriving new possibilities in the future, and when the older person has a sense of renewed purpose and meaning in living and/or dying. Manifestations of these spiritual transformations are unique to the individual person. Expressions of spirituality are shaped by the particular practices and beliefs of culture and religion, as well as feelings, experiences and creative expressions (Labun, 1988). Thomas (1989) believes that healing is the reuniting of the disconnected parts to the whole and occurs within an atmosphere of trust and love, bringing a sense of peace to one's living and/or dying.

Figure 1. A caring model for nursing practice. Scarborough Grace Hospital, Scarborough, Ontario.

Health Care and Spirituality

Traditionally, spirituality has been approached from a one-sided, problem-solving or spiritual distress perspective focusing on the patient's or older person's spiritual problems (Berggren-Thomas and Griggs, 1995). Operating from a fix-it raison d'etre, spiritual problems are labelled and actions specified to rectify the problem. The underlying assumption is that health care providers can resolve the older person's spiritual distress. Little attention is given to the nature of caring relationships and the need for connectedness between the older person and others (including a higher being). Resolution, transformation or transcendence, however, needs to happen within the older person. The fix-it perspective needs to change to a caring ethic that is centred on the nature of the relationships between provider and older person rather than on problem identification and solutions.

Recently, there is a shift toward embracing spirituality as an unfolding, evolving journey within the context of the lived experience (Berggren-Thomas and Griggs, 1995). Experiences belong to the individual. The uniqueness of human nature means that spirituality is experienced by individuals in different ways. Transformative caring means that health care providers choose to accompany the older person through their experiences. The health care provider does not attempt to reframe experiences as problems, but works with the older person to understand and gain insight into their lived experiences.

Spirituality has personal relevance for health care providers as well. Helping others requires that health care providers are in touch with their own spirituality and inner life. The dimensions of the caring relationship take on new meaning when providers can identify with the notions of turning inward, surrender, commitment and struggle in their own lives. In one study, nurses' spiritual well-being found to be significantly ($p < .001$) related to attitudes toward providing spiritual care for patients (Cimino, 1992). These are stressful times in health care. It is imperative that health care providers attend to their own needs for healing and self-transcendence as well as those of their patients. Spirituality can enlarge the purpose and meaning of our lives and work. The actions of care, comfort and healing flow naturally from care providers who have strong interpersonal relationships, peaceful inner lives, and are in touch with their own spirituality.

Caring Relationships and Spirituality

Caring relationships between providers and older persons must be based upon trust, respect and confidentiality. Respect for personhood requires that health care providers take into account particular attributes, needs and abilities of the older person. Culture, education, health beliefs, significant life experiences, hopes and dreams, and social supports are examples of attributes of both care providers and older persons that significantly influence caring relationships.

In urban multicultural settings, language differences between providers and older persons may be initial barriers to the establishment of transformative caring relationships. Language, both verbal and nonverbal, is the way health care providers and older persons come to know each other. Knowledge of the older person gained through translation services of family members or other staff frequently does not permit the same level of intimacy necessary to establish trust and confidence. Despite this barrier, caring relationships do evolve through expressive nonverbal caring processes. Within particular contexts or settings, older persons' needs and abilities will influence the nature of the caring relationship. For example, providers involved with older patients in emergency or ambulatory settings need to establish a trusting relationship in a shorter period of time. Whereas in long-term-care settings, caring relationships can develop over time. Each setting has unique barriers to transformative caring relationships. Relationships of short duration do not provide adequate opportunities to really know the older person as an individual. In long-term settings, there is the danger of complacency and the assumption of "knowing what is best" by the care provider. Regardless of setting, the nature of the caring relationship between health care providers and older persons needs to be the primary focus. When caring relationships are carefully initiated and nourished, the climate that supports respect for person, human dignity and worth flourishes despite the pervasiveness of ageism within the health care system.

A caring relationship consists of three elements: receptivity, relatedness and responsiveness (Noddings, 1984). Receptivity requires a willingness to engage in relationship. Within relationships there is a need for mutuality, trust and confidence. Relationships take time and patience to nurture. With older persons, sensory deficits and slower reaction times may impact on their abilities for receptivity to others. Historical cohort experiences such as wars, may influence the expression of biases and prejudices and obstruct the building of relationships. Many older persons shun health care providers because they fear placement in long-term-care facilities. Older persons with cognitive deficits may also exhibit disinhibition, suspiciousness or mistrust. Authentic caring, however, can transcend these initial barriers to engaging in caring relationships. Through specific tailored approaches, sensory deficits and even paranoia can be overcome. For example, an inexpensive sound amplifier can be used with older persons with hearing deficits who do not have or refuse to wear a hearing aid. Touch, when used appropriately, can be a powerful way to convey concern.

A calm reassuring presence helps a care provider to connect with an older person who is cognitively impaired. For these individuals, a sense of personal connection or affect often remains intact long after speech has been lost. Becoming aware of our own responses and capacities to access our own peaceful-centre is very important (Thomas, 1989). For busy healthcare providers, taking "one minute breaks" to relax and breathe calmly and deeply between interactions with patients and residents is helpful. Regular practices such as prayer, meditation and relaxation exercises are also beneficial in helping health care providers to reflect a warm compassionate manner.

The second element of the caring relationship is relatedness, which addresses the rhythm and paradoxical nature of relationships. As humans relate, they experience at once the paradox of both separating and connecting, revealing and concealing, and enabling and limiting (Parse, 1981). True caring relationships demand involvement, not distance, on the part of the care providers. Benner (1984) has identified deep involvement as one of the characteristics of expert nurses in their relationships with patients. Relatedness in our caring relationships also requires patience and flexibility. Care providers need to understand the ebb and flow of how older persons reveal and conceal their innermost thoughts, dreams and desires. Providing opportunities for older persons to express these dimensions through art, music and literature is important particularly in long-term settings. Group work using reminiscence may help older persons to relate to their past, present and future. Pet therapy demonstrates how unconditional love by an animal influences the well-being and self-esteem of elders in institutional settings (Erickson, 1985). Relatedness is an important aspect of the caring relationship through which the care provider helps the older person to celebrate his or her life.

The last component of the caring relationship that is identified by Noddings (1984) is responsiveness. This element of the relationship involves the duties and obligations of commitment that arise in the caring ethic. Responsiveness entails the selection of caring processes that can be used to help older persons gain insight into their spirituality. The first caring process is coming to know the older person and where he/she is in the spiritual life. Knowing another is an important way to understand unique responses and patterns. Knowing means that the care provider is open and unbiased in responding to the needs of the older person. Knowing is also important as a response to the lived experience of the older individual. Ways of knowing may include: thoughtful discussions of the older person's spiritual assumptions, beliefs, practices, experiences, goals and perceived needs (Forbes, 1994). Encouraging life review and reminiscence, eliciting cherished hopes and dreams, and exploring sources of hope are other ways of coming to know the older person. Gaining an understanding of how the older person has transcended difficulties throughout his or her life is also important in coming to know him/her as a person.

Another caring process that is important in terms of responsiveness is being present to the older person. Presence may be all that is needed, and is often best conveyed by silence and/or touch (Forbes, 1994). Within transformative relationships, the care provider does not provide the answers but rather allows the older person to discover his or her own meanings and beliefs. Active listening is an important element in being present. It means that the care provider is attentive to the older person's body language and affective expressions. It may simply mean that we are able to connect in some small way—a smile, direct eye contact or touch—that makes the human-to-human part of our relationships come alive.

Providing support and encouragement is another way that caregivers can engage in caring processes and transformative relationships. Understanding the older person's family constellation and social-support network is very important, especially the ways that these relationships may have changed as a result of relocation or placement in an institutional setting.

Care providers can also guide and support older persons by understanding and providing for privacy and solitude, particularly when institutional rooms are shared between older persons. Providing an enabling environment for older persons to participate in worship and other religious practices is also very important. Prayer, meditation, reading spiritual literature and imagery are additional ways that can help older persons gain a greater sense of inner peace and meaning in their lives. Finally, true transformative caring can only occur when care providers are open to receiving from those to whom they minister.

Caring Outcomes

The nature of the relationships between care providers and older persons has provided a focus for discussing how spirituality can transform caring. True caring outcomes are apparent when older persons have been actively involved in all decisions related to their care to the best of their abilities, and when desired results are achieved. Human wholeness is never fully attained. Rather, life is the experience of constantly growing and becoming. Affirming life for persons of all ages occurs within the context of one's relationship with a higher being, self, community and the environment (Baxter, 1985). Helping older persons to affirm these relationships is the key to transformative caring.

REFERENCES

Barron McBride, A. (1993). Managing chronicity: The heart of nursing care. In S. Funk, E. M. Tournquist, M. T. Champagne, and R. A. Wiese, (Eds.) *Key aspects of caring for the chronically ill–Hospital and home.* New York: Springer.

Baxter, R. (1985). *Elders and ministry.* Toronto: Anglican Book Centre.

Benner, P. (1984). *From novice to expert.* Menlo Park, Calif.: Addison-Wesley.

Berggren-Thomas, P. and Griggs, M. J. (1995). Spirituality in aging: Spiritual need or spiritual journey. *Journal Gerontological Nursing,* 21(3), 5–10.

Brennan, C. L. and Missine, L. E. (1980). Personal and religiosity of the elderly. In J. A. Thorson, and T. C. Cook Jr. (Eds.) *Spiritual well being of the elderly.* Springfield, Ill.: Charles C. Thomas.

Bianchi, E. (1982). *Aging as a spiritual journey.* New York: Crossroad.

Bohuslawsky, M. (1989). *End of the line–Inside Canada's nursing homes.* Toronto: James Lorrimer.

Buber, M. (1947). *Between man and man.* New York: MacMillian.

Burkhardt, M. A. (1989). Spirituality. An analysis of the concept. *Holistic Nursing Practice,* 3(3), 69–77.

Cimino, S. M. (1992). *Nurses' spiritual well-being as related to attitudes toward and degree of comfort in providing spiritual care.* Unpublished doctoral dissertation, Boston College, Boston.

Erickson, E. J. (1968). Generativity and ego integrity. In B. L. Neugarten (Ed). *Middle age and aging.* Chicago: University Press.

Erickson, R. (1985). Companion animals and the elderly. *Geriatric Nursing,* 6(2), 92–96.

Forbes, E. J. (1994). Spirituality, aging and the community dwelling caregiver and care recipient. *Geriatric Nursing,* 15, 296–301.

Frankl, V. (1967). *Man's search for meaning.* New York: Pocket Books.

Haase, J., Britt, T., Coward, D., Leidy, N., Penn, P. (1992). Simultaneous concept analysis of spiritual perspective, hope, acceptance and self-transcendence. *Image,* 24(2), 141–47.

Hirst, S. and Metcalf, B. (1984). Promoting self-esteem. *Journal Gerontological Nursing,* 10(2), 72–77.

Hungelmann, J., Kenkel-Rossi, E., Klassen, L. and Stollenwerk, R. M. (1985). Spiritual well-being in older adults: Harmonious interconnectedness. *Journal Religion and Health,* 24(2), 147–53.

Labun, E. (1988). Spiritual care: an element in nursing care planning. *Journal Advanced Nursing,* 13, 314–20.

Lane, J. A. (1987). The care of the human spirit. *Journal Professional Nursing,* 3, 332–37.

Nelson, P. B. (1990). Intrinsic/extrinsic religious orientation of the elderly. Relationship to depression and self-esteem. *Journal Gerontological Nursing,* 16(2), 29–35.

Noddings, N. (1984). *Caring: A feminine approach to ethics and moral education.* Berkley: University of California.

Parse, R. R. (1981). *Man-living-health.* New York: Wiley.

Peterson, E. A. (1985). The Physical...the spiritual. Can you meet all of your patient's needs? *Journal Gerontological Nursing,* 11(10), 23–27.

Peterson, E. A. and Nelson, K. (1987). How to meet your client's spiritual needs. Journal Psychosocial Nursing, 25(5), 34–39.

Pieper, H. C. (1981). Church membership and participation in church activities among the elderly. *Activities, Adaptation and Aging,* 1(3), 23–29.

Reed, P. (1987). Spirituality and well-being in terminally ill hospitalized adults. *Research in Nursing and Health,* 10, 335–44.

——. (1992). An emerging paradigm for the investigation of spirituality in nursing. *Research in Nursing and Health,* 15, 349–57.

Roach, S. (1984). *Caring: The human mode of being, implications for nursing.* Caring Monograph. Toronto: University of Toronto.

Rogers, M. (1970). *An introduction to the theoretical basis of nursing.* Philadelphia, PA: F. A. Davis.

Scarborough Grace Hospital (1995). *A caring model for nursing practice.* Scarborough, Ontario.

Thomas, S. A. (1989). Spirituality: An essential dimension in the treatment of hypertension. *Holistic Nursing Practice,* 3(3), 47–55.

Watson, J. (1988). *Nursing: Human science and human care, a theory of nursing.* New York: National League for Nursing.

Walk in Beauty: Aesthetics, Caring and Spirituality

Carol Picard

Movement is what creates life.
Stillness is what creates love.
To be still and still moving—
this is everything.

Do Hyun Choe

Nursing is a profession characterized by *doing*. Nurses' action-oriented use of clinical judgment skills with a focus on doing for patients and their families is a highly valued service to society. A common complaint of nurses is, "So much to do and so little time in which to do it!" This paper will address the need for *being* as well as *doing* in nursing practice. Choe's quote above speaks to the need *to be* as well as *to do* to create a harmony or balance of life in general. This stillness creating love or caring is the ability to be with *other*. While experiences shared in this paper arise out of nursing situations, the human sensitivity called for applies to every human interaction, especially in helping relationships.

Being is a state of awareness, a waking up, an alertness to one's experience in the world. It is the opposite of going through the motions. Being is the path to the sacred, a way to honor the spirituality in everyday acts. In this state of awareness, we notice and attend to our world in a way that integrates the physical and spiritual. But as in the practice of mindfulness in eastern religious traditions, this is difficult to sustain because the mind tends to wander away from the present toward distractions. Being fully present to the moment is difficult, so nourishment

149

and discipline are needed. Hildegard of Bingen, medieval mystic, poet and musician, advises us to nourish our state of being, our inner life, to keep it green, moist and rich. (Hildegard of Bingen, 1985). This is *viriditas,* which enables the person to sustain a *being* presence in the world. As spirituality is nourished and kept green we are present to the moment with *other.* This element of presence is an integral component of caring.

Being and Caring

Sally Gadow (1980) has presented to nursing literature the concepts of lived body experience and object—body experience as a dichotomy felt by the patient in clinical encounters. The lived body experience is that which comprises the history and private reality of being in one's body. The object—body is a conceptualization of the body as a functional object which can be explained and described by an observer. This is observation from a distance, a dispassionate, "objective" approach, in which personhood is lost. Much of what concerns patients today in health care encounters is not having their own experience of hospitalization validated; instead, the problems often could be subsumed under the category of being treated as "object-body"— being talked about in their presence, their concerns unacknowledged, no one inquiring about their needs, believing they were treated only as a body, not as a person. This clinical approach can aggravate or contribute to a person's suffering. Caring requires attending to, being with the patient's lived body experience as patient and person. Being with requires attention, compassion, focus and courage. This is no easy task. Developing this state of awareness and holding it necessitates a nourishing soul diet of experiences for healers.

Nourishing the State of Being: Aesthetics

One form of nourishment, a spiritual vitamin, is aesthetic experience. According to *The American Heritage Dictionary* (1994), aesthetics is "the branch of philosophy which examines the nature and expression of beauty" and "relates to the appreciation of beauty" (p.14). It is coming to know something through our senses and appreciating the beauty of it. Peggy Chinn, in her book *Aesthetics and Nursing Practice* (1994), believes aesthetics "brings forth inner spirit—the essence of human imagination." (p.20). The arts and poetry are usually where we look for aesthetic expressions. In twentieth-century mainstream health care, the aesthetic is rarely integrated into healing practices, except in hospice. But in some healing ceremonies of indigenous peoples in our own country, aesthetics and care of the sick are always paired. The end of the Night Chant ceremony in the Navaho tradition addresses the importance of beauty in life:

> In beauty   I walk
> with beauty before me
>   I walk
> with beauty behind me
>   I walk
> with beauty all around me
>   I walk
> it is finished in beauty.
>   *(Bierhorst, 1984, p. 330)*

Beauty or aesthetics is an important component of the concept *hozho*, meaning life, order and balance to the Navaho. (Ramsey, 1991). They believe in the wisdom of healing the spirit and the body, of appreciating the meaning of the illness for the person, and honoring the lived experience of being as patient and person promotes healing. This may be different than curing. Rather, it is the ability of the person to feel a sense of connection to the healer, the community and the worlds of the spirit and the physical, which is integral to treating patients in the Navaho tradition. There is a Native American proverb which says, "Into each day of suffering there should be equal amounts of beauty." Native Americans believe poetry and dance and art are crucial to recovery and health promotion. This is an integrated healing model.

Thomas Moore in his book *Care of the Soul* (1992) believes the soul is nurtured by beauty. Whether it be the arresting moment of an interpretive dance about loss, or the beauty of a metaphor in a poem, or the feeling captured in a piece of art which makes us stop and catch our breath, we are held by beauty, and soul nourishment occurs. Moore believes beauty invites contemplation. Through aesthetics we come to know the truth of human experience.

Art's Capacity to Heal

Mike Samuels, a physician, in his essay "Art as a Healing Force" (1994), believes art is the voice of the spirit and that "all art, prayer, and healing come from the same place, the human soul" (p.66). It is not only the Navaho who find healing power in beauty. In the spring of 1995, the bombing of the federal building in Oklahoma City became a national tragedy. People all over the world watched as rescuers, nurses, physicians and firemen worked to find survivors and victims of the blast. Two artists, Michael Townsend and Erica Duthie, requested permission from authorities to create a mural for the rescue team. They designed this artwork on the wall of the Myriad Center, the headquarters for rescue operations. In the mural were thirty winged figures taking flight, and at the base of the mural were people who were helping to make the wings. The mural was their gift to the workers. The response of the rescue team was dramatic. Firemen hugged the artists , sharing how they saw themselves as the wing-makers in the picture, helping to set the victims free. Some shared that they would hold the image of the mural in their minds as they began their daily search, and that this imaging helped them with this most difficult work. (Keough, 1995).

The DeCordova Museum in Lincoln, Massachusetts, mounted an exhibit in 1994 called *Body and Soul: Contemporary Art and Healing*. This display featured work by nineteen artists intended to heal viewers, art as expressions of the artists' own healing, art about the healing process and artist-designed healing environments. This highly successful show drew the general public, patients with life-threatening illnesses and caregivers. As a nurse, I was struck with the power of these works to speak to the viewer about illness, suffering, healing and wholeness. Each artist's being, his/her sense of beauty and soulfulness, was evident in every work, and uniquely so.

The aesthetic, then, offers us a different perspective on human experience, particularly in illness. We appreciate the mystery of life and realize that a mechanistic, problem-solving approach may, if isolated, contribute to the patient's suffering. *Being with* is as important as *doing for.*

Poetry as Aesthetic Language

Daniel Gioia, author of *Can Poetry Matter?* (1992), defines poetry as the "art of using words charged with their utmost meaning" (p.20). Poetry illuminates the truth of an experience. Often poetry brings together things which are usually apart through the use of metaphor to surprise us into the beauty of contemplation. The poet approaches experience from a totally different viewpoint than the clinician. Here are two examples of contrast in the clinical and poetic languaging of an experience of a comatose patient on a respirator:

Example 1:

A. General Nursing Assessment:

Neurological:	Pt. comatose. No response to verbal command or deep painful stimulation. Pupils fixed and dilated. ICP >30 torr. CPP 20 Mannitol 25 Gm given q 6 hr. Awaiting results from EEG and flow scan.
Respiratory:	Ventilator set at ac/16. PEEP of 5. FI02 100% Tidal volume 800. No spontaneous respirations. No cough or gag reflex. Suctioned q 3 hr. for minimal clear white secretions. Bilateral breath sounds w/ equal chest expansion. Coarse ronchii at the bases.
Cardiovascular:	Heart rate 80. Sinus rhythm w/ occasional PAC's. B/P 130/80. IV N/S at 200cc/hr. B/P 130/80. IV N/S at 200cc/hr. Skin warm and dry. Color pink. Good capillary filling of nailbeds. No breakdown areas noted.

Gastrointestinal: Abdomen soft. No distention. Good bowel sounds. N/G tube placement checked. Draining moderate amount of dark green drainage. Guiac neg. pH 6. No stool.

Genitourinary: Foley to bedside drainage. Clear yellow urine. SG 1.005. Urine output > 300//hr.

Social: Family support provided. Aware of patient's condition. Visiting with patient.

House officer notified and aware of patient's condition throughout shift.

B.

> *Seeing Fred On a Respirator*
> Oh God
> I will never take breath,
> breathing, blowing a kiss, a candle
> for granted again.
> The breath
> Take a breath
> The in breath
> The out breath
> The infinite possibilities
> of what we can do with
> the gift of breath.
> What we take in first on our arrival
> and the last we give up on returning to
> that place without the rhythm of breath.
> *(Picard, 1992)*

Example 2:

A. Home visit for dressing change to ulcer on r. leg. Stage 2 decubitus measuring 1x 1 1/2cm Drainage serosanguinous. NS wash followed by duoderm dressing. Taught wife and daughter dressing care. Wife is scheduling podiatrist visit. Pt. having angry outbursts frequently and unable to make needs understood due to expressive aphasia. Family members anxious about how to handle this. Referred wife to agency support group.

B.

Pepere's had a shock
His fist comes down to meet yellow formica
in his daughter's cramped kitchen.
Damn! Damn! Damn!
He wants to say pencil, water, baby, but what comes is
Damn!

Silent Henry, a Lincoln-like figure with a shock of black hair,
even at sixty-six.
Family stories of a quiet man who said little
all his life.
He was precise, as when measuring and leveling
the foundation of this house he now stands in.

After his stroke,
all the words in his head clamor to get out
demanding passage over his tongue, through his mouth,
a launch at the lips.
They are turned back, prisoners.

Words of affection, sadness, joy,
wonder, and regret.
Only Damn!

He pounds formica, with a carpenter's surety,
hammerless.

(Picard, 1994)

What is so different about each pairing? The clinical notes are in the third person, with little reference made to anything but valuable, observable data. This is important information about object-body orientation to the patient. The poems are focused on the unique experience of the nurse in the first poem, and the patient in the second. What the reader can derive from the poems is an aspect of caring which Mayeroff (1971) calls "alternating rhythms": by using a particular situation we can also keep the generalities of the experience of all patients and nurses. In fact, I would expect the readers to reflect on their own lived experiences when contemplating these poems.

Heart to Heart: Aesthetics and Daily Practice of Caring

What role can aesthetics play in the daily life of the care-givers? Beauty, as the Navaho know, has the capacity to heal both the sick and the healer. Aesthetics can offer both a personal source of spiritual nourishment and a different kind of way to link "heart to heart" with those being cared for. Oncology/hos-pice nurses and caregivers have much to teach about the role of beauty in patients' lives. In my visits to oncology floors in hospitals and to hospice centers, including one in Moscow, the presence of art in the daily life of the patient creates an environment which heals not only the spirit of the patient but that of the nurse.

Aesthetics as the language of the heart is easily available in clinical settings if nurses choose to use it. Sharon DiVitto worked as a trauma nurse on a helicopter team for many years and believed in the power of music to heal. When she would be sent to transport a patient from one hospital to another, she carried with her a selection of musical tapes of every type. She would ask patients, where possible, to select their favorite music for the short-but anxiety-producing ride to the trauma center. She noted an effect on vital signs as a result. (*Personal Communication*). Kathy Panagiotes in her work as a nurse manager, regularly played music such as Pachelbel's Canon at the noon hour on her unit as a heal-ing period for staff and patients. Preparing oneself to care is more than preparing one's body for work. (Panagiotes, *Personal Communication*, March 2, 1993).

Being in the Midst of Doing

Liz Shilale, an emergency room nurse, uses the beauty of daily centering prayer and notes its effect on her practice in this vignette: on a particularly busy winter evening, an elderly man was brought to the emergency room and died of a heart attack. As Liz cared for a person on the bed next to the deceased, she heard through the curtain someone say to the elderly wife, "Don't worry, you'll get over it." As soon as she was able, she went to the widow, touched her shoulder, and said to her, "I am so sorry for your loss. As you can see we are very busy tonight, but I have a little time and I'd like you to tell me something about your husband. I can stay with you for five minutes. Tell me." As the woman wove several small stories together, she was pulling herself together. When Liz had to leave to meet the helicopter with an accident victim she told the woman again that she was sorry for her loss, thanked her for sharing the beautiful stories and said, "Even though I can't stay with you, I know you are here, and I'll keep an eye on you." As she worked she would often look to the corner of the room and nod to the grieving woman who would close her eyes and nod back. (Shilale, *Personal Communication*, January 12, 1995).

Creating Art/ Patient as Artist

If patients kept journals of the lived experience of their illness which became part of the clinical record, we would have a wealth of rich information and a truer, convergent picture of what is happening to the person would emerge. The patient would have an opportunity to reclaim his/her body while in the clinical setting and prevent becoming over-medicalized. An artist shared the experience of having her husband lying comatose in a nursing home following surgery for a brain tumor. When the nursing staff one day shaved his mustache for convenience sake without consulting her, she felt the only aspect of his personhood which existed for her was his visage and now this had been robbed. She proceeded to draw a portrait of him and create a poster which she placed at the head of his bed. She wrote a message on the poster: "This is my husband." She wrote little anecdotes about his life and interests, and invited the staff to add to the poster. Her goal was to create an artistic statement about the person who lay in the bed as a way of helping not only herself but the staff who had difficulty not seeing him as object-body.

One does not have to be Picasso or T.S.Eliot to create aesthetic expressions. An invitation to create is often the catalyst a person needs to begin. The following poem is a meditation on the needs of a family:

One Hospital/Two Worlds
The elevator door opens
and they move in as one.
Old K-Mart parkas, worn but durable
in the faded colors of many washings.
The three, two sisters and a young son.
The lines of the mother's face
etched on the young boy's brow.
He presses 6.

The mother's red-eyed fatigue comes from worry, yes,
and from having no partner to roll with
in the rhythm of sleep.
Making the bed so simple, one hand smoothes the covers
the right side looking freshly made, night or morning.

She takes the picture from her pocket,
the one I think the nurses asked for:
"Bring us a picture of your husband when he was well."
Fishing pole, his beaming grin and belly fills the camera lens,
as he hoists the wide mouth bass to the sky.
The young son is running in
from the margins of the picture, blurred,
too late to be part of this captured, still moment.

Nurses from five get on at two,
chatting about baby showers and cafeteria fare,
as interns' talk of cardiac rounds
punctuates this moving room.
But in their bubble these three hear nothing
but the sound of the ICU's machinery
and someone's breathing two floors up.

(Picard, 1992)

The nurses in the poem understood the need to have an image of the healthy person in his room, both for them and for the family. In my work as a psychiatric nurse, I often invite the patients to use both the works of others to contemplate their own experiences, and to write, draw, photograph, make collages and listen to music as a path to knowing what their inner spirits need. Frequently people will use a journal to write narratives, poems, and do sketches during therapy. One's creative impulse is nourished by taking in the works of others. Sharing favorite readings, cards, poems, selecting artwork for unit walls and suggesting aesthetic experiences to patients can help. They are searching. Spend time in any bookstore and one can hear conversations between persons with illnesses and bookstore owners as they search for resources to help in their healing process.

Nurse as Artist

Parker (1992) explored the effect of being an artist—creating beauty in craft—on a person's nursing practice. The impact on the artist's practice of nursing was to enhance the experience of being. As she states, "My art and my nursing meet, touch and overlap in being together....There are spiritual, transforming elements in my actions....There is a connection with what has been missing on some level. I am healed. My patients are healed" (Parker, p.33).

Doing can get in the way of being. Spending time in a creative activity demands settling down and focusing on being. As one artist put it, "When I am creating, I have to just be still and get out of the way of the creative impulse." This discipline in centering and being, carries over into work with patients. Preparing oneself to care is more that preparing one's body.

Sharing poems, quotes, cards, books, photographs with patients and families, and inviting them to share the same with us validates the importance of beauty and aesthetics in healing. And of course, there is the creative work itself. In my practice, I have used poetry as a way to come to understand my patients' experiences. In sharing the poems with patients, in each instance, the response has been one of enthusiasm for feeling truly understood in their struggle to be whole. The following is an example of an aesthetic way of validating the patient's experience:

> Land's End
> You are running for your life
> at the end of the world

where rock-solid and firm meet
the force of waterwaves.

You are standing your ground
As your family, like
the steel gray ocean
persists, demands
pulls at you.
The seductive rhythm of the waves
persistent, relentless
the force of it, especially
when whipped by a storm.

The salt of the water
is the salt of your blood,
the magnetic pull of the pole.
Sometimes, I've heard, rivers change direction.

You build a hut by the shore,
sturdy if small
and the waves beckon with
a fearful regularity.
Calling, pressure and call,
the chorus of voices
on the surface calling,
pulls at you
"Don't build so far up"

If you heed the voices,
when others run by in the morning
only sticks and a running shoe
will be left for their dogs
to find in the morning rain.

                       (Picard, 1993)

    Another creative work involved two poems about patient's experiences which were choreographed and performed for both nursing groups and the public. This work entitled, "On Caring," was well received because the themes of each particular poem relate to many persons' experiences with vulnerability and feeling invisible in their experiences as patients.

Conclusion

Aesthetics offers caregivers and those we care for a pathway to transcendence, the capacity to go beyond the self. By nourishing our appreciation for beauty we nourish a soulful way of being in the world with each other. Being and doing must be in balance in order to have a caring relationship with *other*. Aesthetics can contribute to and inform caring practice in the creative work of artists, patients and nurses. All have the capacity to contribute to the integration of body and spirit in communion with each other, in the ability to walk in beauty.

REFERENCES

American heritage dictionary. (1994). 3rd ed. New York: Bantam.
Bierhorst, J. (1984). *Four masterworks of American literature.* Tuscon: University of Arizona Press.
Chinn, P. and Watson, J. (1994). *Art and aesthetics in nursing.* New York: National League for Nursing.
DiVitto, S. (April 5, 1995). *Personal Communication.*
Gadow, S. (1980). Existential advocacy: Philosophical foundations of nursing. In S.Spicker and S. Gadow, (eds.). *Nursing images and ideals.* pp.86–101. New York: Springer.
Hildegard of Bingen. (1985). *Illuminations of Hildegard of Bingen.* Santa Fe: Bear and Co.
Keough, J. (1995). Hope takes wing in Oklahoma City. *Holden Landmark* May 25, pp. 23–25.
Mayeroff, M. (1971). *On caring.* New York: Harper Collins.
Moore, T. (1992). *Care of the soul.* New York: Harper Perennial.
Panagiotes, K. (March 2, 1993). *Personal Communication.*
Parker, M. (1992). Exploring the aesthetic meaning of presence. In D.Gaut (ed.). *The presence of caring in nursing.* pp. 25–37. New York: National League for Nursing.
Picard, C. (1992). Seeing Fred on a respirator._*Nightingale Songs,* February 4.
——. (1993). Land's end. Unpublished poem.
——. (1994). Pepere's had a shock. *Bay State Nurse News* 3:5.
——. (1996). One hospital/two worlds._*Baystate Nurse News,* March, 2.
Ramsey, J. (1991). Poetry and drama in healing: The Iriquoian *Condolence Ritual* and Navaho *Night Chant. Literature and Medicine* 8 pp. 78–99.

Samuels, M. (1994). "Art As A Healing Force." In *Body and Soul: Contemporary Art and Healing.* Lincoln, MA: DeCordova Museum.

Shilale, E. (January 12, 1995). *Personal Communication.*

(The author would like to thank Sharon DiVitto for her suport in the preparation of this essay.)

Illuminating the Meaning of Caring: Unfolding the Sacred Art of Divine Love

Marilyn A. Ray

Abstract

Caring is identified as distinctively human, a human mode of being and becoming. Dwelling more deeply with the nature of caring shows us that the foundation of caring is love and subsequently a spiritual way of being. This chapter addresses the relationship between love and caring by presenting an inquiry into love and caring as a sacred art. The chapter briefly illuminates the philosophical history of the idea of love and uses the profession of nursing as an illustration of this sacred art. Communion with the "other" or the "compassionate we" forms the foundation from which an understanding of God as the Mystery of Being in the caring relationship is presented. Illuminating the meaning of caring as love is a transformative experience wherein the constant birthing of love in caring actions is the growth of the spiritual life within. Knowledge of the unfolding of inner wisdom and the inner mystery of participatory life will serve to engender a new sense of awe related to the mystical dimension of the call in the healing and helping professions that has been lost in contemporary culture.

Introduction

Caring has been identified as distinctively human—a human mode of being and becoming (Roach, 1987; Boykin and

163

Schoenhofer, 1993). Recently, in the caring profession of nursing, a new vision has been shaped by focusing on nursing as caring (Leininger, 1981). As the caring paradigm is becoming more rooted in the consciousness of nurses (Watson, 1985; Roach, 1987; Eriksson, 1989, 1992; Newman, Sime, Corcorran-Perry, 1991; Appleton, 1991; Boykin and Schoenhofer, 1993; Ray, 1994a), there is now a call for nurses to dwell more deeply with the nature of caring to understand and communicate its inner structure. Eriksson (1992), a leading theorist in European nursing, remarked that "[t]rue caring is not a form of behavior, not a feeling or a state. It is an ontology, a way of living. It is not enough to be there, to share—it is *the* way—the spirit in which it is done" (p. 209). Eriksson (1992) proclaimed that caring is an expression of *caritas*—human love and charity. In a philosophical analysis of care and caring in nursing, Ray (1981) revealed that caring was synonymous with love and was grounded spiritually by the living out of a vision of compassion for others that has been characterized in the Judeo-Christian Scriptures. Kelsey (1981) and Roach (1987) similarly pointed out how caring is a feature of the theology of love, wherein caring concern for others enables the coming of wholeness in human beings so that they may achieve their eternal destiny of union with God. A closer examination of the meaning of caring as love and as a sacred art is the purpose of this chapter. A brief overview of the idea of love, historical perspectives of love, and love as caring will be presented. A discussion of love through caring in the profession of nursing as the sacred art of love, and the meaning of the ontologic structure as the spiritual unfolding of divine love will ensue.

The Idea of Love

Love is a spiritual, transcendent power that knows, understands and has its own wisdom and science by its knowledge of the inner mystery of participatory life (Merton, 1985). Love transforms. It reveals our true purpose, identity and deep personal meaning. Love calls forth our deepest creative power to appreciate "life as value and gift" (Merton, 1985). We are by nature united by a primordial empathy (Stein, 1989). This empathy is becoming the other in mind and heart—loving the other's interests (Dubay, 1973). Buber comprehended this connectedness as a dialogical, spiritual intersubjectivity—the I-Thou relationship (Buber, 1987; Friedman, 1976). The relational is thus spiritual; it is the life of the Beloved (Nouwen, 1995). The participating consciousness of the human being is, as Marcel (Spiegelberg, 1982) illuminated, a "we are" where relational human beings participate in Being (the Creator) in a spiritual sense and manifest themselves as a response to the Thou (Buber 1987). This participatory "we are," or mystery of God as love, enables the expression of concrete actions of compassion and caring.

All major religions speak of the significance of love. The Hebrew and Christian Scriptures tell us that God, the Creator, is love, and a covenant of love was made between God and his people. In Leviticus, we are told to love God and our neighbor as ourselves (Leviticus 19:18, 1995; Kelsey, 1981). A virtuous life is expressed as loving and righteous (the image of God). Within Christianity, love is the supreme ontologic action of the triune God—the Father, Son, and Holy Spirit. Of the theological virtues of faith, hope and love, love is considered the greatest of them all (1 Cor. 13:13, The New American Bible, 1972). Love is present by an inner response to the action of God's grace and love in human affairs (Fox, 1992). The Islamic conception of God as love is expressed in the Al-Qur'an, wherein God is discerned as compassionate and merciful (Jaoudi, 1993), and followers of Islam engage in works of charity for the poor (Kelsey, 1981). "God's action is the perfect expression of love... and [w]hen we love we participate in God's way of reaching out to humankind" (Kelsey, 1981, p. 16). In the mystical religions of the east, for example, Hinduism, Taoism, and Buddhism, the transcendent way of compassion is expressed in concern and caring for others (Ray, 1994b). Love, thus, is central and participates in creation through concrete actions of caring because there is divine essence, an unfathomable mystery (Fox, 1992).

Historical Perspectives of Love

Throughout history, the philosophy of love is illuminated as virtue, perfection and responsibility to the "other." In premodern times, philosophers apprehended love in terms of the following: teaching and understanding achieved through the mother-child relationship (Socrates, cited in Halliburton, 1981); beauty and the idea of perfection (Plato, cited in Singer, 1987); and human goodness as the activity of the soul (virtuous or ethical activity) (Aristotle, cited in Kaplan, 1958).

In the middle ages, the concept of love was differentiated in two ways: first, between emotional and theological love (love of God), and second, the understanding of love as participatory. Elaborating on Aristotle's notion of virtue as prudence, Aquinas (1967) categorized love in terms of both sense-good and sense-evil. He analyzed love from an intellectual perspective which connected love to goodness governed by reason or choice.

During the renaissance, love was viewed as both religious idealization (love of God) and courtly idealization (romantic love). For example, a man's virtue was expressed by devotion to a woman's beauty of person and of soul (Singer, 1987).

During the last few centuries, love continued to be expressed in the ideal terms of communion with another, and the virtue of fidelity or faithfulness. It was not until modern times that the idea of conflict in love relationships was given expression. Although Shakespeare was well known for his writings of conflictual love, it was Sartre's (1948; Singer 1987) existentialism that was considered a twentieth century reaction to idealistic philosophies of love, especially the philosophies of Buber and Marcel, which Sartre reproached. Enlarging on the concepts of good and evil reflected in Genesis 2 and 3 in the Hebrew Scriptures, Buber, however, recognized that good and evil, as well as awareness of a free response to narcissistic or egoistic motivation, were at work in all human beings (Evans, 1993). In his writings, Marcel (1962), too, recognized a turning away from the love of God by noting a rebellious individuality in the society. Marcel, in turn, criticized Sartre for his lack of acknowledgement of the supernatural, grace and the afterlife. In general, Sartre introduced separateness rather than participation into theories of love—separateness, individualism and the absence of God (Sartre, 1948; Singer, 1987). He argued that the ultimate goodness of being was love as "balanced tension"

(Singer 1987, p. 342). The idea of love as balanced tension, however, was first identified in the Christian Scriptures. Love is commingled with forgiveness. The foundational ethic of Jesus Christ was growth in love—the reconciliation of tension between the duality of the potentiality for sin and the capacity for compassion and love (Sanford, 1988).

Evans (1993) outlined secular views of love and described them as follows: the cynical, in which love is an illusion and in which narcissistic rather than nonnarcissistic motivation is dominant; the conflictual, in which love is real and has to compete equally with narcissism which cannot be eradicated; and monistic, in which love is the most fundamental motivation and in perpetual conflict with narcissism or evil, which in essence does not have a power unto itself. Evans, however, posited his own particular view of love wherein he described love as cosmic and spiritual where the loving energy which pervades the universe must be motivated by human beings. Evans also saw that loving energies could be reversed by narcissistic motivation which are classified as hatred, anxiety, obsessiveness and so forth.

The perception of the universe as cosmic and spiritual is consistent with much of the new paradigm thinking occurring in contemporary religious, philosophical and scientific circles today (Capra, Steindl-Rast with Matus, 1991; Evans, 1993; Moore, 1992). The interest in the idea of a spiritual universe has been steadily increasing in secular realms in recent years. The diminishing sense of a feeling of caring and relatedness in communities and a lack of human belongingness in an age of instant global communication, combined with the tenets of the new science of complexity, have contributed to this concentration (Talbot, 1988; Harman, 1991; Capra, Steindl-Rast with Matus, 1991). For example, in a recent study of the metaphysical reexamination of science, Harman (1991) stated that the new science of complexity indicates that all phenomena of the universe are interconnected and mutually embedded. Harman (1991) posited that just as humans and the world are accepted as mutually embedded, so too, should be science and religion. The split between science and religion is no longer valid. A new paradigm in science now is underway that supports and encourages exploration of wholeness that is all inclusive, that is, that includes all the evidence—physical sense data and intuitive inner knowing (Mayeroff, 1971; Kelsey, 1981; Roach, 1987; Capra, Steindl-Rast with Matus, 1991; Harman, 1991; Ray, 1991; Fox, 1994).

Love as Caring

Love is seen and "tasted" as it is actuated in our way of being through the grace of God, faith and prayer, and by the way we, as human beings, relate to others through caring (Clarke, 1995). This caring way of being also extends to all living creatures and the environment (The New American Bible, 1972; Schuster & Brown, 1994). Love is reinforced through the reading of the Scriptures. The Christian Scriptures demonstrate love as caring by the words and examples of Jesus Christ who manifested the virtues and duties of a life of compassionate love and justice. These loving examples of the Beloved are reenacted by we, who are devoted to God through faith, prayer, and good works, and God's gift of grace to us. God's mercy through grace, thus, is the power that permits the practice of a virtuous and caring life for human beings.

As evidenced in the Scriptures and in ethical analyses throughout history, there always has been interest in the idea of care and its relationship to the moral life and to loving behavior. It is only recently, however, that this concept is being adequately explored. The study of feminine moral development more than anything else was responsible for identifying the magnitude of the importance of caring in contemporary life (Gilligan, 1982). Moreover, Aristotle's vision of love or human goodness as ethical activity that was central to the classical medieval synthesis of the concept of virtue as an "excellence," grounded in natural law, consciously and rationally practiced for the good of others is being revisited (Pellegrino, 1995). The Aristotelian notion of virtue that eroded over the centuries because of little consensus or agreement on a definition of the concept of the good is being reformulated in health care arenas to emphasize the relationship among the person acting, the act and the consequences of the act. The facilitation of morally good decisions that are both technically correct and caring within the healing professions (Pellegrino, 1995) is at a critical stage of evaluation.

Earlier in evolutionary history, however, caring was identified as the central element in the survival of human beings and one of the oldest forms of human expression (Constable 1973; Leininger, cited in Watson 1979). In contemporary philosophy, Heidegger (1962, 1972), claimed that the nature of being in the world was to care. He regarded love and thinking as inclination—prior but obscure knowing. As such, the unconcealment of love is "the opening of presence," that is, what is appropriated—a relation of man and Being. Heidegger (1972) specifically does not reference God in his idea of "the opening of presence." Other Continental philosophers, especially Derrida, decried the idea of presence, whether that was a view of presence as the immanent presence of God, the self as certain, or the world as determinant (Solomon, 1990). At the same time, current psychology illuminated the importance of the presence of love, both psychologically and spiritually, and also its opposite, the presence of evil in individual and social relationships (Peck, 1978). Sanford (1988) claimed that the successful working out of the problem of evil (the shadow side of reality) can only be reconciled in the bonding by love. He pointed out that parents or significant others were ultimately the foundation for a moral life. "...[T]he moral life, in the last analysis, although grounded in theology, comes down to a person's relatedness to people and a capacity for human feeling" (Sanford, 1988, p. 55).

Illuminating the significance of caring as a relational moral activity invokes questions relating to the long-standing emphasis on individualism and patriarchy dominating western culture. Recognition of the benefits of belonging to others and caring for individuals and community has fostered a new understanding of cosmic interconnectedness. An appreciation for cultural diversity, feminine strengths, eastern philosophies of the balance between masculine and feminine energies, and environmental care are taking hold in a global civilization (Fox and Swimme, 1982; Leininger, 1991; Harman, 1991; Schuster & Brown, 1994). As revealed, this awareness is encouraging the dissolution of the traditional patriarchal paradigm that emphasized dualisms in all domains and is facilitating a new integrative image of reality. The split between science and theology has brought forth a new wholism wherein a revisioning of science, religion and the art of living is being made apparent (Fox and Swimme, 1982; Harman, 1991). This spiritual vision that is materializing beholds the connectedness of all the earth and its inhabitants, the cosmos and God into a loving network of relationships (Capra, Steindl-Rast with Matus, 1991). This image acknowledges further the preeminence of the caring image of God in the person of Jesus Christ present in the Bible. The universe is beginning to be recognized as the dwelling place wherein everything is to be revered and understood as connected and considered sacred. The universe now is considered a place where the integrity of God, the Divine Mystery present in all as love, is beginning to be perceived as the primordial energy of the universe (Teilhard de Chardin, 1967; Capra, Steindl-Rast with Matus, 1991; Fox, 1992; Ress, 1993).

The Path Of Love Through Caring In Nursing

Nursing is one of the oldest professions. Patterns of love and concrete caring actions are observable in nursing clinical situations. The current health care system emphasizes economics. Nurses voice concerns for wholistic caring even when corporate voices consider only "bottom line" issues and nurse caring as a liability or a cost overrun. Nurses, however, continue the desire to be compassionate and caring. Nursing is still the beacon for humane care. Inquiry into economics and caring shows that the healing process with patients would be ineffective without nurse-love (Ray, 1987). The call to help, or the call to serve another in nursing as in other helping professions, is a vocation which in its deepest sense is informed by faith, discernment, prayer and listening to the Word of God. "He [God] judges according to what he has heard" (John 5:30; Clarke, 1995, p. 20).

The act of a profession, or a belief in helping a vulnerable other, has been defined by Pellegrino (1995) as "...an act of implicit promise making that establishes a trust at the physician's or nurse's voluntary instigation....The promise made to the dependent patient directs the knowledge, techniques, and personal commitment of the physician or nurse to the *telos* of the relationship—helping and healing" (p. 267). Moreover, love through concrete caring actions shows again that giving without expecting anything in return will yield receiving in more abundance (The New American Bible, 1972; Peck, 1978). This love is illuminated in the following poetic illustrations of nursing:

By the Morning Light
It was eleven at night.
The hospital ward (we called them wards in those days) was dark.
I came into a room where Dr. Paul was standing over the bed of young John who was dying of a severe endocarditis.
Dr. Paul said, "I am glad to see you. I'll leave now and rest."
"I will call you if I need you," I said.
John was hot, flushed and drifting in and out of consciousness.
I talked to him softly, whispering, "We'll work together you and me; you will pull through, you know."
Praying silently and sometimes out loud, I asked God to help—to save him.
I worked with John, alternating cold ice packs with tepid sponge baths.
I managed his intravenous fluids with the medications needed to lower his fever.
The presence of death was looming.
Prayer and compassion were, too.
Talking, praying, soothing, treating; the night was soon day.
By the morning light, John spoke.
His fever had broken. He awoke. I smiled.
We were absorbed in the nearness of love that is nursing.

In the Nearness of Love
In the nearness of love that is nursing, there is a secret sharer—the unmastered thereness of a prior creation realizing itself in the compassionate we.
Choosing to grant to and share in the moments of presence and dialogue, we are moved forward and upward, transformed.
The spiritual presence communicates a depth of felt realness, an authenticity, and integrated wholeness, a call to understand what we have understood.

In the chronicle of professional nursing, Nightingale (1860) was the first to identify nurses' work as charity, as God's work, and equated nurses' love for patients with moral goodness and the image of God. Nursing was built on the foundation of love expressed in motherhood and the religions, especially Christianity. Apart from Nightingale, the inner structure of nursing or nurse-caring as love was not identified until recently (Ray, 1981; Watson, 1985; Swanson, 1990; Appleton, 1991; Halldorsdottir, 1991; Eriksson, 1992; Victor, 1993). In the search for an answer relative to the basic questions about nursing, Eriksson (1992) identified the *caritas* motive (love) as the most prevalent idea to shape nursing throughout its history. The *caritas* motive in nursing has been largely a hidden phenomenon in modern professional nursing circles. It is consistent with Teilhard de Chardin's (1967) commentary that socially, in science, business and public affairs, people pretend not to know love.

Love is the heart of caring and its unifying focus (Ray, 1981). Co-presence or participatory life was identified as essential within the structure of nursing. Caring thus exists as oblative love, a reciprocal giving and receiving in response to a need. Caring is authentic presence, availability, attendance and communication which includes interest, acceptance, touch and empathy (Ray, 1981). The relational oblative loving relationship in nursing is the "compassionate we." Compassion, in this sense, is "a wounding of the heart by the 'other,' where the other enters into us and makes us other" (Ray, 1991, p. 182). This inner life experience forever changes the lives of both the caregiver and the one being cared for. It is similar to what Nouwen called the wounded healer (cited in Roach, 1987) and the life of the Beloved (Nouwen, 1995). In the nursing situation, the meaningful pattern of experience is transformation and transcendence; it is the felt presence, in what Plato referred to as the "aspiration to invisible reality" (Steiner, 1989, p. 223). The profound experience of caring is a mystery, but is practiced and appreciated as a sacred art.

The vision of love as real presence and meaningful to life and well-being opens our eyes to the reality that love is not esoteric or something that should not be talked about in nursing. Responding to the value and reality of lovingness, the nurse is one who, along with the joys, accepts "...simultaneously the consciousness of our human agony...love's anguish of contradictions, conflict and ignorance" (Merton, cited in Cardenal, 1972, p. 15). The sacred art of love, through the concrete actions of caring in nursing and other disciplines dedicated to the care of others, guides according to its own inner truth (Merton, 1985). The dynamic nature of caring as love, thus, manifests our essence—our being. Caring is Love; caring is life itself.

The Unfolding of Divine Love as the Ontologic Structure of Caring

Caring unites body, mind and soul. This treatise fundamentally shows that caring is an ontologic spirituality—the ontologic mystery of Being (Marcel 1949; Marcel, cited in Spiegelberg, 1982). "Ontology is an inquiry into the being [forms or ideas] of something and into its range of possibilities" (Roach, 1987, p. 45). An ontologic spirituality is an inquiry into caring in a spiritual sense, but grasped through the revelation as the mystery of our own being. Thus, the starting point for this inquiry of caring is awareness that caring is mystery, is of God. The process ultimately involves reflection and discernment which "...is the light to know God in knowing ourselves" (Clarke, 1995). An ontologic spirituality, therefore, does not begin with doubt, but with wonder and amazement in the belief that the "I am"—the incarnate being, the body as the content of experience, participates in Being in a spiritual sense (a transcendent Being). The "I am" moves toward the "I belong" in loving participation through sensation and the revelation of Being, the force within and without. What is important is not the "I am," "I exist," or the "I think," but the "we are."

The unique pattern of caring as the sacred art of love attends specifically to the creative and sensitive quality of loving presence within and communion with others. The "compassionate we" is humanly visible (incarnate) and responds to the spiritually invisible (transcendent). In the choice of granting to the other a share in one's being—a spiritual intuition or transcendent knowing is present and at work. The communion with the other of the "compassionate we" is a call to a deeper life of meaning. This call more fully opens us up to the mystery of Being. An affliction endured in common, such as the healing in the illness experience of the patient through the efforts of the nurse in relation to the struggle of suffering and pain fuses a bond, and, as such, permits the bond to arise in the first place. The felt grief is the birth of an indissoluble unity of love that facilitates the coming to know the meaning of meaning—the continual revelation of the mystery of Being by the pouring forth of faith, hope and love. The mystery of the "we are" through the inclination and motive to choose to respond to the invitation, and response to care by the giving and receiving of love is constantly being revealed. In both the believing and unbelieving consciousness, the participatory "we are" is none other than a sharing in the love of God, the life of the Beloved (Nouwen, 1995).

An ontology of caring as the sacred art of love is first the awareness of love and givenness because there is love, a force which is the basis of all intersubjective or co-present experience (within and between). The compassionate encounter between the nurse and patient by the reciprocal pattern of transformation and transcendence through caring is a supernatural movement which permits in us the ability to become more fully human. "We do not become fully human until we give ourselves to each other in love," stated Merton (1985, p. 27). In loving communion, others show us the secrets of their souls, while at the same time they show us the "secrets of our own souls" (Moore 1992, p. 281). This sacred art imitates our destiny. It reveals the eternal in our everyday lives.

Conclusion

The evolution of the idea of love throughout the ages, and within nursing in particular, through the action of love as caring, culminating in the ontology of caring in nursing as divine love and co-presence, has been presented. Dwelling deeply with love as the motive of caring as a way of being in nursing and communicating its inner structure illuminated its meaning as spiritual, a sacred art. In this analysis, the art of the spiritual in caring action revealed a theology—an awareness of God as love, a felt realness of the Mystery of Being in the "compassionate we" relationship. This creative fidelity of relatedness is a sign of the soul—a pouring forth of faith, hope and love because there is love, the primal energy of the universe. Nursing is, thus, the constant birthing and growth of love, the unfolding of the inner wisdom and inner mystery of participatory life.

REFERENCES

Appleton, C. (1991). The gift of self: The meaning of the art of nursing. *Dissertation Abstracts International* 52–12B, no. 92I5314.

Aquinas, T. (1967). The emotions, *Summa Theologiae*, Vol. 19. (Eric D'Arcy, Trans). New York: McGraw-Hill. London: Eyre and Spottiswoode.

Boykin, A., and Schoenhofer, S. (1993). *Nursing as caring: A model for transforming practice.* New York: National League for Nursing Press.

Buber, M. (1987). *I and thou.* (R. Smith, Trans). New York: MacMillan (Originally published 1958).

Capra, F., and Steindl-Rast, D., with Matus, T. (1991). *Belonging to the universe.* San Francisco: HarperSanFrancisco.

Cardenal, E. (1972). *To live is to love.* Garden City, N.Y.: Image Books.

Chardin, Teilhard de. (1967). *On love.* New York: Harper and Row Publishers.

Clarke, T. (1995). Discerning through the senses. *Weavings: A Journal of the Christian Spiritual Life,* 10(6), 16–26.

Constable, G., and Editors of Time Life Books. (1973). *The Neanderthals.* New York: Time Life Books.

Dubay, T. (1973). *Caring: A biblical theology of community.* Denville, N.J.: Dimension Books.

Eriksson, K. (1989). Caring paradigms: A study of the origins and the development of caring paradigms among nursing students. *Scandanavian Journal of the Caring Sciences* 3(4), 169–176.

Eriksson, K. (1992). Nursing: The caring practice—"Being there." In: *The presence of caring in nursing.* D. Gaut (Ed.). New York: National League for Nursing Press.

Evans, D. (1993). *Spirituality and human nature.* Albany: State University of New York Press.

Fox, M. (1979). *A spirituality named compassion and the healing of the global village; Humpty Dumpty in us.* Minneapolis: Winston Press.

——. (1992). *Sheer joy.* San Francisco: HarperSanFrancisco.

——. (1994). *The reinvention of work.* San Francisco: HarperSanFrancisco.

Fox, M., and Swimme, G. (1982). *Manifesto! For a global civilization.* Santa Fe: Bear and Company.

Friedman, M. (1976). *Martin Buber: The life of dialogue*. Chicago: The University of Chicago Press.

Gilligan, C. (1982). *In a different voice*. Boston: Harvard University Press.

Halldorsdottir, S. (1991). Five basic modes of being with another. In D. Gaut and M. Leininger (Eds.), *Caring: The compassionate healer*. New York: National League for Nursing Press.

Halliburton, D. (1981). *Poetic thinking: An approach to Heidegger*. Chicago: The University of Chicago Press.

Harman, W. (1991). *A reexamination of the metaphysical foundation of modern science*. San Francisco: The Institute of Noetic Sciences.

Heidegger, M. (1962). *Being and time*. (J. MacQuarrie and E. Robinson, Trans). New York: Harper and Row Publishers.

——. (1972). *On time and being*. New York: Harper and Row Publishers.

Jaoudi, M. (1993). *Christian and Islamic spirituality*. New York: Paulist Press.

Kaplan, J. D. (1958). *The pocket Aristotle*. New York: Washington Square Press.

Kelsey, M. (1981). *Caring: How can we love one another?* New York: Paulist Press.

Leininger, M. (1979). Foreward. In J. Watson, *The philosophy and science of caring*. Boston: Little, Brown and Company.

——. (Ed.) (1981). *Caring: An essential human need*. Thorofare, N.J.: Slack, Inc.

——. (Ed.) (1991). *Cultural care diversity and universality*. New York: National League for Nursing Press.

Leviticus. *God's Word Today*, 17(9), 4–50.

Marcel, G. (1949). *The philosophy of existence*. New York: Philosophical Library.

——. (1962). *Homo viator*. New York: Harper and Row Publishers.

Mayeroff, M. (1971). *On caring*. New York: Harper and Row Publishers.

Merton, T. (1972). Foreward. In E. Cardenal, *To live is to love*. Garden City, N.Y.: Image Books.

——. (1985). *Love and living*. (N. Stone and P. Hard, Eds.). San Diego: Harcourt, Brace, and Jovanich Publishers.

Moore, T. (1992). *Care of the soul*. New York: Harper Collins Publishers.

New American Bible. (1972). New York: Catholic Book Publishing Company.

Newman, M. A., Sime, A. M., and Corcorran-Perry, S. A. (1991). The focus of the discipline of nursing. *Advances in Nursing Science*, 14(1), 1–6.

Nightingale, F. (1860). *Notes on nursing*. New York: Appleton and Co.

Nouwen, H. (1995). *Life of the beloved*. New York: Crossroad.

Peck, M. S. (1978). *The road less traveled: The psychology of spiritual growth.* New York: Simon and Schuster.

——. (1983). *People of the lie: The hope for healing human evil.* New York: Simon and Schuster.

Pellegrino, E. (1995). Toward a virtue-based normative ethics for the health professions. *Kennedy Institute of Ethics Journal,* 5(3), 253–57.

Ray, M. A. (1981). A philosophical analysis of caring within nursing. In M. Leininger (Ed.), *Caring: An essential human need.* Thorofare, N.J.: Slack, Inc.

——. (1987). Health care economics and human caring in nursing: Why the moral conflict must be resolved. *Family and Community Health,* 10(1), 35–43.

——. (1991). Caring inquiry: The esthetic process in the way of compassion. In D. Gaut and M. Leininger (Eds.), *Caring: The Compassionate Healer.* New York: National League for Nursing Press.

——. (1994a). Complex caring dynamics: A unifying model of nursing inquiry. *Theoretic and Applied Chaos in Nursing,* 1(1), 23–32.

——. (1994b). Transcultural nursing ethics: A framework and model for transcultural ethical analysis. *Journal of Holistic Nursing,* 12(3), 251–264.

——. (1994c). Communal moral experience as the research starting point for health care ethics. *Nursing Outlook,* 42(3), 104–109.

Ress, M. (1993). Cosmic theology: Ecofeminism and panentheism, Brazilian feminist theologian Ivone Gebara. *Creation Spirituality,* 9(6), 9–11.

Roach, S. (1987). *The human act of caring.* Ottawa: The Canadian Hospital Association.

Sanford, J. (1988). *Evil: The shadow side of reality.* New York: Crossroad.

Sartre, J. P. (1948). *The emotions: Outline of a theory.* New York: The Wisdom Library.

Schuster, E., and Brown, C. (Eds.). (1994). *Exploring our environmental connections.* New York: National League for Nursing Press.

Singer, I. (1987). *The nature of love: The modern world* (3). Chicago: The University of Chicago Press.

Solomon, R. (1990). *Continental philosophy since 1750: The rise and fall of the self.* New York: Oxford University Press.

Spiegelberg, H. (1982). *The phenomenologic movement: A historical introduction.* The Hague: Martinus Nijhoff Publishers.

Stein, E. (1989). *On the problem of empathy.* 3rd revised ed. Washington, D.C.: ICS Publications.

Steiner, G. (1989). *Real presences.* London: Faber and Faber.

Swanson, K. (1990). Providing care in the NICU: Sometimes an act of love. *Advances in Nursing Science*, 13(1), 60–73.

Talbot, M. (1988). *Beyond the quantum*. Toronto: Bantam Books.

Victor, B. W. (1993). Theoretical discussion of a model of caring for persons with HIV infection. *Scandinavian Journal of the Caring Sciences*, 7(4), 243–50.

Watson, J. (1985). *Nursing: Human science and human care. A theory of nursing*. Norwalk, Conn.: Appleton Century Crofts.

The Convergence of Caring and Spirituality: Gandhi, An Exemplar

Sarla Sethi

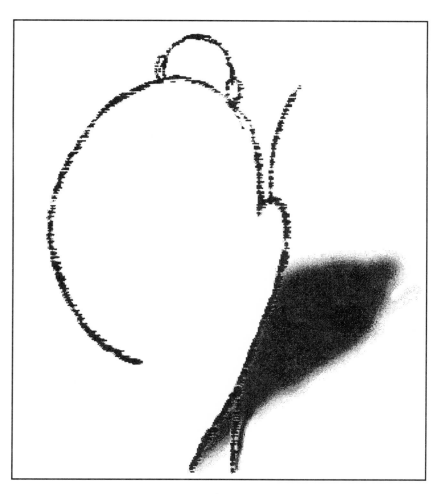

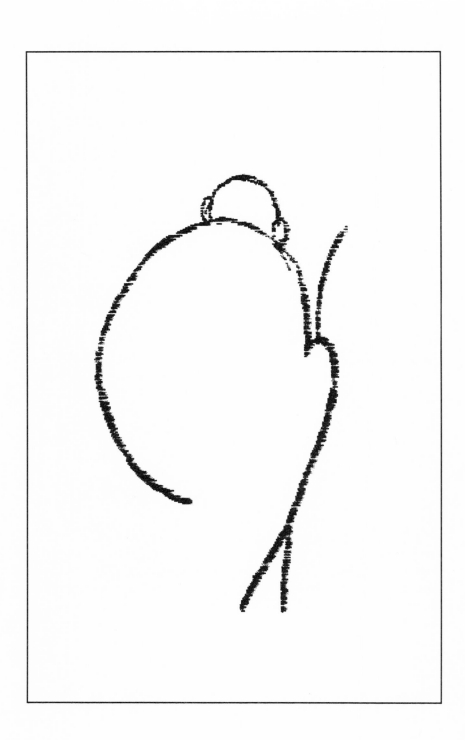

Why be proud
Of being big
If it serves
No noble purpose!

Like a date tree
Tall and useless,
Without a foliage
It provides
No shelter
To the weary traveler,
And its fruit
Is so much out of reach!
Kabir

Like a date tree, a person's life is useless if it is lived only to serve oneself. This kind of existence, one that pursues success, prosperity and the luxuries of life only to satisfy personal desires, conveys a lack of passion for, and an inability to comprehend, our interconnectedness in humanity. "The true value of a human being is determined primarily by the measure and sense in which [a person] has attained liberation from the self" (Einstein, 1979, pp. 7-8). A liberated person portrays an inmost sense of spirituality. Spirituality is an expression of the wholeness of the person; it is an internal dynamic force, which propels the person to transcend reality and the self (Buscaglia, 1978; Trungpa, 1985).

Selected Views On Spirituality and Caring

Some traditions believe that for spirituality to be fully realized, a person needs to turn away from the world. This view is isolating. Spirituality is not just a religious phenomenon. Spirituality is an integration of all conduct of human living (Schneiders, 1986). Ochs (1983) affirms that, "spirituality is not merely a way of knowing, but also a way of being and doing: 'All real living is meeting' " (p. 10). In order for a person's spirituality to mature, a person needs to be in a relationship with reality— experiencing human conditions from human perspectives. During caring moments, one's spirituality is lived. Gandhi said:

"I do not believe...that an individual may gain spiritually while those around him suffer.

...I believe in essential unity of man and for that matter, of all that lives. Therefore, I believe that if one man gains spiritually, the whole world gains with him and if one man falls the whole world falls to that extent". (Cited in Attenborough, 1982, p. 23)

Living a life away from reality results in a lack of sensitivity to human ills and the causative social conditions responsible for those ills.

Spirituality is discernible in a person by the development of abilities to embrace all kinds of life; to respond to the needs of the fractured world around us; and to attend to the pleas and plights of all human beings with compassion (Puls, 1985). Puls' statement, "It is the heart of our efforts to be human. It is the seamless robe worn in all our roles," (1985, p. 1) describes the essence of spirituality. Spirituality is expressed in its highest form when a human being is "living an ordinary life extraordinarily well" (Chittister, 1990, p. 6).

The ordinary life lived extraordinarily well happens when an individual responds to all human conditions intentionally and in a caring manner, and finds significance and meaning in the lives of all people. The spiritual person experiences the world and, in a concrete sense, the surrounding society as his/her community. Gandhi's search for the "supreme soul" was accomplished by immersing himself fully in the affairs of humanity. He moved out of himself to be in relationship with others and with their concerns. Gandhi asserted:

I am a part and parcel of the whole, and I cannot find Him apart from the rest of the humanity. My countrymen are my nearest neighbours. They have become so helpless, so resourceless, so inert that I must concentrate on serving them. If I could persuade myself that I should find Him in a Himalayan cave, I would proceed there immediately. But I know I cannot find Him apart from the humanity, (Cited in Prabhu and Rao, 1946, p. 30)

Gandhi reflected his spirituality in his actions as a caring human being. According to Mayeroff (1971), "through caring, a man lives the meaning of his own life" (p. 6). Caring is expressed by accepting people's diverse realities without being dogmatic or judgmental, and by assisting others without possessing: "I experience what I care for as having worth in its own right" (p. 6).

Watson (1985) describes caring as a means of protecting, enhancing and preserving human dignity rather than as an end in itself. She states that caring is the vehicle that will allow for the realization of the innermost spirituality for both the caregiver and the one cared for. Through acts of caring and being cared for, they will find meaning in their existence and experiences and discover inner powers of self-healing. Participation in caring requires person-to-person engagement at personal, social, moral and spiritual levels, "a commitment to oneself and other humans" (p. 25). Caring creates possibilities in the midst of the most deprived circumstances.

Benner and Wrubel (1989) believe that caring is an enabling condition that sets up the possibility of giving and receiving help; and caring means being connected and having people, events and things matter . Caring is actions that nurture; actions that foster growth, recovery, health and protection of those who are vulnerable (Benner and Wrubel, 1989). Gadow interprets caring as "the commitment to alleviating another's vulnerability" (1988, p. 6). Caring is to take charge of the protection, welfare, or maintenance of something or someone in a manner that enables one to find one's own meaning and create one's own integrity (Noddings, 1984 and Gadow, 1988). This means empowering the cared-for.

Roach (1992) states that caring—the human mode of being—can be demonstrated through the five C's of compassion, competence, confidence, conscience and commitment .

THE ATTRIBUTES OF CARING

Compassion

According to Roach compassion is "a way of living born out of an awareness of one's relationship to all living creatures; engendering a response of participation in the experience of another; a sensitivity to the pain and brokenness of the other; a quality of presence which allows one to share with and make room for the other" (1992, p. 58). A compassionate person alleviates the pain of friends and strangers alike. Nouwen (1994) views the compassionate human being as one who is able to immerse her/himself in the condition of the other in an unpretentious manner. Fox captured the heart of compassion: "It is loving ourselves while we love others. It is loving the possibilities of love and survival. It is one love that permeates all" (1990, p. 33). With compassion one becomes a colleague in humanity.

Competence

Competence reflects caring in a person who conscientiously acquires and uses appropriate knowledge, skills, experiences, motivation and energy in assisting another person to grow fully (Roach, 1992). Roach was very clear about the importance of being competent in a caring relationship. She asserts that "while competence without compassion can be brutal and inhumane, compassion without competence may be no more than a meaningless, if not harmful, intrusion into the life of a person or persons needing help" (p. 61). A caring person has a well-developed array of cognitive, affective, technical and administrative skills, and uses these skills in a manner that assists another person to experience growth and self-actualization.

Confidence

Confidence is a crucial attribute of caring because it fosters trusting relationships of mutuality (Roach, 1992). Confidence in one's ability to care for others is evident when a person creates unknown, untested possibilities in which others can realize growth in themselves. Confident caring enables others to take risks and to find meaning in their own lives. Caring confidence is not paternalistic; it empowers others to reach their desired goals .

Conscience

Conscience "is a state of moral awareness; a compass directing one's behavior according to the moral fitness of things" (Roach, 1992, p. 63). A person who truly cares acquires the knowledge and skills needed to deepen moral understanding so that he or she responds appropriately to the moral and ethical issues faced by self and others

Commitment

Commitment is "a complex affective response characterized by a convergence between one's desires and one's obligations, and by a deliberate choice to act in accordance with them" (Roach, 1992, p. 65). Commitment is devoting oneself fully in such a manner that ensures that caring will happen in a situation (Mayeroff, 1971). A caring person is persistent in maintaining and promoting caring occasions.

Patterns of caring attributes reflect the nature of a person's spirituality. This nature is reflected in the patterns of caring—how she/he demonstrates the attributes of caring in action. "Spirituality is the way we express a living faith in a real world" (Chittister, 1990, p. 4). These five attributes illuminate the ontological competencies of caring, and are cited here as attributes reflected in the life of Mahatma Gandhi. Gandhi's spirituality was expressed in his way of living, in his relationships with all people including his oppressors, and in his identification with the suffering of his own people.

Mahatma Gandhi, An Exemplar

Human caring and spirituality converge in the life and practices of Mahatma Gandhi. Against a background of selected works on spirituality and caring, Gandhi is presented as an exemplar who in his everyday concerns, relationships and political activities, showed what it means to be a spiritual person. Gandhi transcended the self and the evils of unjust domination by manifesting nonviolence and love for all people. He passionately modeled a compassion that responds to the spiritual hunger of our time.

Mahatma Gandhi (named Mohandas Karamchand Gandhi) was born in a Hindu family in India, on October 2, 1869. Mahatma means "great soul." He is known universally as the one who struggled, using nonviolent ways, to gain independence for India from Britain. To the Indians he was known as "Bapu," or father.

In his autobiography Gandhi (1957) stated that his devoutly religious mother and his nurse taught him to speak the truth under all circumstances and not to fear reprisals. These teachings left a lasting impression on him; as did the following stanza, originally written in Gujarati language .

> For a bowl of water give a goodly meal;
> For a kindly greeting bow thou down with zeal;
> For a simple penny pay thou back with gold;
> If thy life be rescued, life do not withhold.
> Thus the words and actions of the wise regard;
> Every little service tenfold they reward.
> But the truly noble know all men as one,
> And return with gladness good for evil done. (Gandhi, 1955, p. 8)

"Return good for evil" became Gandhi's guiding principle. Gandhi's faith in the equality of religions grew as a result of listening to discussions between his father and his Moslem, Parsi and Jain friends. Gandhi formed his views about his personal relationships with others by paying close attention to the teachings of his parents and of his nurse, and by questioning the justification of certain practices. Gandhi not only questioned but he also acted to resolve social and political evils by vigorously pursuing solutions to improve the human condition (Sharp, 1979).

Bhattacharyya states that a reader of Gandhi's life must attend to his conscience (1969). His "Conscience manifests itself in terms of sensitivity to sufferings and injustices, to rights and wrongs. In a sense, conscience is authoritative" (p. 17). Gandhi's life is best described as a life of service. He believed in extending himself to nurse the sick, the wounded, and to heal the afflicted without any reservations. Gandhi said:

Whenever you are in doubt or when the self becomes too much with you.... Recall the face of the poorest and most helpless man you have ever seen and ask yourself if the step you contemplate is going to be of any use to him. Will he be able to gain anything by it? Will it restore to him control over his life and destiny? In other words, will it lead to self-rule for the hungry and spiritually starved millions of our country-men? Then you will find your doubts and self melting away. (Cited in Attenborough, 1982, p. 25)

Gandhi believed in experimentation for the purposes of discover-ing "truth." Relying on his conscience from boyhood, Gandhi dis-regarded conventions and customs even if it meant going against the established "mores of the society and against the scriptural injunctions of his people" (Mazumdar, 1963, p. 14). For example, Gandhi and his friends questioned the Hindu practice of not eat-ing meat. Gandhi's young mind surmised that, in order to achieve political freedom, the Indians of Hindu faith required physical strength to match the beef-eating, burly Englishmen. He thought that if Hindus incorporated meat in their diets, they would gain the necessary strength to free India from the British Raj. Gandhi's experiment with eating meat was short-lived because he realized that he could not ethically subscribe to a practice which also meant hiding truth from his mother. Mazumdar (1963) describes Gandhi's character by stating:

...the experiment of meat-eating came to an end, but it showed the mettle of the boy; he was willing to try out what his conscience told him was right and was bold enough to discard his previous judgment if later experience proved to him that it had been wrong. (P.14)

Gandhi completed his law studies at the Inner Temple in London, and then returned to India to pursue his legal career (Mazumdar, 1963). In India, he was hired by an Indian company having legal transactions in South Africa and was asked to relo-cate to South Africa for a year. According to Rao (1968), "the cir-cumstances in South Africa conspired to bring out the best in Gandhi" (p. 155), evolving the values, inspirations and spiritual beliefs that guided his life.

The turning point of Gandhi's career came when he was traveling in a first class compartment on a South African train. A white man objected to sharing the compartment with a person of color (Gandhi, 1936). Gandhi refused to move and was thrown out of the train. The injustice of this incident inspired him to fight color discrimination, and to struggle for the freedom of the oppressed people in South Africa (Fischer, 1954). Singh (1990) states:

> Gandhi drifted away from legal practice. He appeared in the courts not as an attorney but as an accused person. In the twenty-one years he spent in South Africa (1893-1914), he was imprisoned four times and on many occasions manhandled by the police and by his own countrymen. The South African experience made Gandhi turn to pacifism. (Pp. 163-64)

It is in South Africa, Gandhi developed his strategies to fight the exploiter, the ruling class (Chandra, 1972). He developed strategies of *ahimsa* (nonviolence), *civil disobedience* and *satyagraha* (truth-force) to disarm the oppressing force. Gandhi proclaimed nonviolence as the greatest and the most active force in the world (Nelson, 1971). His aim was to transform nonviolence, a cloistered virtue, into an active social instrument (Rao, 1968). He stressed activism and stated that "one cannot be passively nonviolent" (Gandhi, 1936, p. 114).

Satyagraha means adhering to truth in order to fight injustice. Pyarelal labeled Gandhi's approach as the "diplomacy of truth" (1965). The satyagraha method was to erect a human wall that will resist coercion and invasion, and will refuse to yield to the usurper. Gandhi sometimes called *satyagraha* a "struggle of the right against the might" or a "soul force" pitted against "brute force," and emphasized that this included *civil disobedience* (Chandra, 1972, p. 85). Gandhi said *satyagraha* is "vindication of truth not by infliction of suffering on the opponent but on one's self" (cited in Fisher, 1954, p. 35). Gandhi was adamant that the goal of eradicating injustice was not achieved by illegal means such as law-breaking tactics, but rather by noncooperation and disciplined strikes.

Gandhi's teachings have touched people from all walks of life. Passionate in his attempt to awaken the inner strengths of people to become self-respecting human beings, Gandhi's actions and words taught people to have pride in themselves and to feel worthy as human beings. He emphasized kindness, honesty, humility, nonviolence and the exaltation of the human spirit as a way of living (Fischer, 1954). He showed to the peoples of the world how to become caring human beings, how to value all other persons regardless of their color, class, religion or gender and how to pursue equality of opportunity. His maxim was protection and enhancement of human dignity under all circumstances. Gandhi was compassionate toward all people:

> I cannot intentionally hurt anything that lives, much less human beings even though they may do the greatest harm to me and mine. While, therefore, I hold British rule to be a curse, I do not intend to harm a single Englishman or any legitimate interest he may have in India. (Cited in Gold, 1983, p. 82)

Gandhi's views on the practice of untouchability is a testimony of his compassion and conscience. Gandhi said:

> I regard untouchability as the greatest blot on Hinduism. Untouchability has degraded us, made us pariahs of the [British] empire. What crimes, for which we condemn the British Government as satanic, have not we been guilty of crimes towards our untouchable brethren. (Cited in Singh, 1990, p. 165)

Gandhi decried the discriminatory practices of the Hindu people that prevented the untouchables from using public institutions because of their social class. Even in his early years Gandhi argued with his mother against observing untouchability in relation to the family sweeper. Despite objections from the Hindu orthodoxy, Gandhi invited an untouchable couple to become members of the *Ashram* (community) in which he lived. He referred to untouchables as "Harijan," children of God, and was determined to adhere to his goal of eradicating the practice of untouchability. His actions and determination resulted in the abolition of untouchability and its practice in any form in the newly formulated Constitution of India in 1950. The acceptance of the Constitution meant that all Indians, including the untouchables, would have equal access to all public facilities, for example, temples, parks, recreational complexes and public institutions such as schools and universities. (Although the practice of untouchability was abrogated in public places, it took almost four decades before the practice of untouchability was abolished by the people of India in their private lives.) Gandhi's caring acts were those of a compassionate person who relieved the "pain of fellow creatures by way of justice-making" (Fox, 1979, p. 34).

To free India from British rule, Gandhi displayed full commitment to the principles of *ahimsa, satyagraha* and *civil disobedience.* He believed in serving India's and Indians' interests by being conscious of the effects that his actions could have on India and other countries. Gandhi emphasized, "I want the freedom of my country so that other countries may learn something from my free country, so that the resources of my country might be utilized for the benefits of mankind" (cited in Sharp, 1979, p. 178).

The Rowlatt Acts, passed on March 18, 1919, allowed judges to try political cases without juries and to jail political suspects without due process. Gandhi responded to this decision by initiating a day of fasting and prayers; in effect this was a general national strike (Gold, 1983). At a protest meeting on April 12, 1919 in Jallianwallah Bagh in the Punjab region, British troops killed 379 Indians because they had disobeyed the proclaimed ban on public meetings. Gandhi responded to this tragedy through noncooperation and organization of a boycott of British goods and schools, and even British jobs.

Gandhi, however, was always amenable to any conciliatory British gesture that might have brought a peaceful conclusion to the issue at hand, because he considered that a sign of progress. He would willingly reverse any course of action to allow for a satisfactory resolution. For Gandhi, "to trust is a virtue" (Gold, 1983).

One of Gandhi's greatest victories was the Salt March. According to Gold (1983) even though India had the resources for salt production, the British monopolized the production and marketing of salt, making it difficult for Indians to make salt for local or home consumption. Indians had to pay a tax to their British rulers each time they bought salt. To fight this injustice, Gandhi organized a march to protest this practice on March 2,

1930. He wrote to the British Viceroy stating his intention to organize a massive campaign of *civil disobedience:*

> I know that in embarking on nonviolence I shall be running what might fairly be termed a mad risk, but the victories of truth have never been won without risks, often of the greatest character. Conversion of a nation that has consciously or unconsciously preyed upon another far more numerous, far more ancient, and no less cultured than itself is worth any amount of risk.
>
> I have deliberately used the word 'conversion.' For my ambition is no less than to convert the British people through nonviolence and thus make them see the wrong they have done to India. I do not seek to harm your people. I want to serve them even as I want to serve my own. (Cited in Gold, 1983, p. 82)

The Viceroy forewarned Gandhi that this course of action was in violation of the law and hence could endanger public peace. Gandhi's reply was: "I repudiate the law, and regard it as my sacred duty to break the mournful monotony of the compulsory peace that is choking the heart of the nation" (1951, p. 85).

Gandhi was committed, regardless of the consequences, to improving the lives of his people. He had a sound knowledge of the salt issue and full confidence in his ability to mobilize the masses in a huge campaign of civil disobedience. Even though the Salt March ended as a bloody battle, Gandhi's actions helped Indians to unite in their rejection of bad laws. Gandhi demonstrated attributes of competence and confidence in stating:

> I believe I have rendered a service to India and England by showing in noncooperation the way out of the unnatural state in which we both are living. In my humble opinion, noncooperation with the evil is as much a duty as is cooperation with good. (Cited in Gold, 1983, p. 77)

On August 15, 1947, India became an independent nation. The struggle against the British Raj ended. Subscribing to the principle of secular humanism and firmly believing that the "cornerstone of the freedom of India is Hindu and Muslim unity" (Gandhi, 1921, p. 541), Gandhi made every attempt to stop the division of India on the basis of religious beliefs. Gandhi was instrumental in gaining India's independence from Britain, but he was unable to prevent the partition of the Indian continent into two separate countries: India and Pakistan. Because of the partition, a widespread civil war ensued. This tarnished the achievement of a peaceful transition to *Swaraj* (self-rule). Sorensen (1968) states that Gandhi "failed to recognize how the noblest intentions can become deplorably mistranslated by those who have not the requisite spiritual endowment" (p. 367).

When Gandhi realized that the partition of India was unavoidable, he fervently appealed to Hindus and Muslims to stop the killing and to refrain from violence. Regrettably, the civil war escalated. Discovering that his plea was ignored, he decided to "fast unto death" unless the war between Hindus and Muslims stopped. He was unwavering in his adherence to the principles of nonviolence and the truth-force, making every effort within his power to assure protection and enhancement of human dignity during this transition.

Gandhi acknowledged the participation of women was crucial in the creation of a just society (Joshi, 1988), and was uncompromising about women's rights (Rao, 1968). Gandhi said "In my opinion, [a woman] should not labour under any legal disability not suffered by a man" (cited in Joshi, 1988, p. 19). According to Gandhi, the social practice of dowry in an Indian society, for example, was nothing but the sale of girls. He said, "If I had a girl under my charge, I would rather keep her maiden all her life than give her in marriage to one who demanded even a pie as a condition for marrying her" (Joshi, 1988, p. 196). Gandhi believed in gender equality of the sexes, and advocated the same rights for women as for men.

Gandhi was a supreme exemplar of a caring "inspired by the vision of humanity evolving toward a world of peace and harmony" (Martin Luther King Jr., cited in Attenborough, 1982, book cover). Gandhi's life and actions manifested compassion for all living beings, a knowledge of human conditions, confidence in his ability to make a difference, adherence to moral values of nonviolence under all circumstances, and a goal of equality for all. Serving a noble purpose, Gandhi addressed social evils with both humility and determination.

Conclusion

The spirituality of a person is comprehended by studying his/her patterns of caring acts in the world. Puls (1985) states that "spirituality embraces all life, breathes through its homely details and its noble intentions" (p. 1). Responsive to all human beings and their conditions, Gandhi advocated adherence to the principles of *satyagraha* (truth-force) and *ahimsa* (nonviolence).

Satyagraha and *ahimsa* generate tolerance, promote personal growth and stimulate the evolution of a caring being. Gandhi's life and teachings build an awareness of the greatness of human potential in changing a disconsolate human condition to one that is filled with hope, dignity and opportunity. Through caring—exercised through compassion, competence, confidence, conscience and commitment—a human being can alleviate the suffering of others. A spirituality of caring creates possibilities for constructing a just world for all. Gandhi's life was like an oak tree full and wide—unlike a date tree, sparse and narrow. His actions affected the lives of millions of common people, providing solace and warmth, and restoring dignity in people and helping people to find meaning in their lives.

> I recognize no God except the God that is to be found in the hearts of dumb millions...And I worship the God that is Truth...through the service of these millions. (Gandhi, cited in Pyarelal, 1965)

Mahatma Gandhi gained independence for Indians from Britain without firing a single bullet. He was killed by a bullet. He died a violent death as he nonviolently challenged the injustice of a violent political system.

REFERENCES

Attenborough, R. (1982). *The words of Gandhi*. New York: Newmarket Press.

Benner, P., and Wrubel, J. (1989). *The primacy of caring: Stress and coping in health and illness.* Menlo Park, Calif.: Addison-Wesley Publishing Company.

Bhattacharyya, B. (1969). *Evolution of the political philosophy of Gandhi.* Calcutta: Calcutta Book House.

Buscaglia, L. F. (1978). *Personhood: The art of being fully human.* New York: Ballantine Books.

Chandra, V. (1972). The evolution of *satyagraha* in South Africa. In D. K. Misra, S. L. Doshi, and C. M. Jain (Eds.), *Gandhi and social order* (pp. 80–89). Delhi: Research Publications in Social Sciences.

Chittister, J. (1990). *Wisdom distilled from the daily: Living the rule of St. Benedict today.* New York: HarperCollins Publishers.

Einstein, A. (1979). *The world as I see it.* Secaucus, New Jersey: Citadel Press.

Fischer, L. (1954). *Gandhi: His life and message for the world.* New York: New American Library.

Fox, M. (1979). *A spirituality named compassion.* Minneapolis: Winston Press.

———. (1990). *A spirituality named compassion.* New York: HarperCollins Publishers.

Gadow, S. A. (1988). Covenant without cure: Letting go and holding on in chronic illness. In J. Watson, and M. A. Ray (Eds.), *The ethics of care and ethics of cure: Synthesis in chronicity* (pp. 5–14). New York: National League of Nursing.

Gandhi. M. K. (1921). *The collected works of Mahatma Gandhi (1921).* Publication Division, Ministry of Information and Broadcasting, Government of India. San Francisco: Harper SanFrancisco.

———. (1936). Non-violence in peace and war. *Harijan,* 1, 113–16.

———. (1951). *Satyagraha: Non-violent resistance.* Ahmedabad: Navajivan Publishing House.

———. (1955). *My religion.* Ahmedabad: Navajivan Publishing House.

———. (1957). *An autobiography: The story of my experiments with truth.* Ahmedabad: Navajivan Publishing House.

Gold, G. (1983). *Gandhi: A pictorial biography.* New York: New Market Press.

Joshi, P. (1988). *Gandhi on women: Collection of Mahatma Gandhi's writings and speeches on women.* Ahmedabad: Navajivan Publishing House.

Kumar, S. (1984). *The vision of Kabir: Love poems of 15th century weaver-sage.* Concord: alpha & omega.

Mayeroff, M. (1971). *On Caring.* New York: Harper and Row.

Mazumdar, H. T. (1963). *Mahatma Gandhi: A prophetic voice.* Ahmedabad: Navajivan Publishing House.

Nelson, W. S. (1971). Gandhian values and the American civil rights movement. In P. F. Power (Ed.), *The meanings of Gandhi* (pp. 153–63). Honolulu: The University Press of Hawaii.

Noddings, N. (1984). *Caring: A feminine approach to ethics and moral education.* Berkeley: University of California Press.

Nouwen, H. J. M. (1994). *Here and now: Living in the spirit.* New York: The Crossroad Publishing Company.

Ochs, C. (1983). *Women and spirituality* Totowa, N.J.: Rowman and Allanheld.

Prabhu, R. K., and Rao, U. R. (1946). *The mind of Mahatma Gandhi.* London: Oxford University Press.

Puls, J. (1985). *Every bush is burning: A spirituality for our times.* Mystic, Conn.: Twenty-third Publications.

Pyarelal. (1965). *The last phase.* Ahmedabad: Navajivan Publishing House.

Rao, K. R. (1968). *Gandhi and pragmatism.* Calcutta: Oxford and IBH Publishing Company.

Roach, M. S. (1992). *The human act of caring: A blueprint for the health professions.* (Rev. Ed). Ottawa: Canadian Hospital Association press.

Schneiders, S.M. (1986). Theology and spirituality: Strangers, rivals, or partners? *Horizons,* 13(2), 253–74.

Sharp, G. (1979). *Gandhi as a political strategist.* Boston: Porter Sargent Publishers, Inc.

Singh, K. (1990). *India: An introduction.* New Delhi: Vision Books.

Sorensen, E. (1968). Great soul. In S. Radhakrishnan (Ed.), *Mahatma Gandhi 100 years* (364–68). New Delhi: Gandhi Peace Foundation.

Trungpa, C. (1985). Ego and spiritual materialism. In J. Garvey (Ed.), *Modern spirituality: An anthology* (pp. 117–23). Springfield, Ill.: Templegate Publishers.

Watson, J. (1985). *Nursing: Human science and human care.* Norwalk, Conn.: Appleton-Century-Crofts.

Developing Spiritual Care: The Search for Self

Gwen Sherwood

There is a resurgent need for spiritual explanations for coping with the uncertainties, catastrophes, crime and loss so prevalent in the world. For most of us, there is a certain mystery counter-balanced with longing which surrounds spirituality and spiritual care. Relegated to professional chaplains, ministers, and nuns, most health care professionals experience discomfort when the conversation turns inward for a look at the soul. Regardless of religious persuasion, we have failed to develop an awareness or the skills needed to address spiritual needs. Most health care systems give spiritual care a lower priority even though evidence suggests it may have a positive effect on recovery (Stiles, 1990). To effectively offer spiritual care to others, we must first begin the search for our own self-identity. My work with both graduate and undergraduate nursing students has generated strategies grounded in caring from the heart in the search for meaning and purpose.

Caring and Spirituality

We all have a spiritual dimension. The heart is the ground of the soul, our core or apex of our being. It forms the center for decision making or our intentionality of action, our thought processes, the action center as well as our reflecting center. It is the center of our caring being, our humanness which reaches outward towards others (Roach, 1992). Caring gives rise to our meaning and purpose for being in the world (Frankl, 1959). Caring forms a useful foundation for exploring our spirituality. Concepts of spirituality link the holism of health care to the

196

inseparable interconnections among humans defined by caring (Watson, 1988). Grounded in permanent values and moral imperatives, caring has a certain dynamic in human interactions which flow between and connect the caregiver and care receiver. This mutual, relational process is the satisfaction caregivers experience in caring interactions, contributing to a sense of meaning with purpose in their work (Sherwood, 1992).

The caring process can activate a higher power, order or energy in the universe which potentiates healing, health, and self-knowledge (Keegan, 1995). The caring process goes beyond basic competency toward higher-level, professional-care processes which augment health and healing. Caring theory demonstrates how the various parts relate to the whole (Sherwood, 1995).

Examination of Gaut's (1986) philosophical approach to caring shows three basic relational statements fundamental to caring: (1) There must be an identified need for care. (2) The caregiver must know what needs to be done to address the need and do it. (3) There must be intent for the intervention to serve as a means for positive change in the other. Gaut's analysis shows caring as intentional knowing leading to action. That is, caring from the heart uses our reflective knowing, our cognitive thoughts and our action center to create positive outcomes for the other.

Such intimate caregiving, regardless of professional background, requires the caregiver to a self-evaluation of spiritual concerns. The question arises, then, of how to work with students, health care professionals or other caregivers to develop the spiritual care of our being? It is essential if we are to care for the whole person, to go beyond just the physical and psychosocial. The challenge is how to bring this center, this soul, to the surface of who we are and how we present ourselves in the world. How do we become whole, living an integrated life?

Awareness and Knowing

Boyd's (1988) model of the modes of awareness is an underlying foundation for exploring the authentic, integrated self. It is through our modes of awareness that we develop our capacity to interpret the experiences which make up our lives. In using the arts and humanities for a health care process in a humanitarian paradigm, we draw on our many modes of awareness: moral, beliefs, spiritual, esthetic, intuitive, historical, judgment, scientific, common sense, empathic, dreams, remembrance and imaginative. All help develop and define our inner selves.

Another way to examine the search for our spiritual self is by applying the four ways of knowing identified by Carper (1978): physical, aesthetic, ethical and personal. The *physical* way of knowing involves the logical, thinking self, the science of caregiving; however, the rational can never fully account for what it is to be human, to have uniqueness. While this is the most familiar and generally most valued way of knowing in health care, there are other ways which stretch and further define the full capacity of what it is to enter a caregiving relationship.

The **aesthetic** way of knowing involves the art of caregiving, empathy, presence, being with the other. The compassionate nature of caregiving is expressed through the aesthetic, creative self.

The **personal** way of knowing utilizes one's mental or emotional self. It is standing in relation to the other; the I/thou relationship. There is reciprocity in the emotional way of knowing through the actualized moment—each individual alone yet working together.

The **ethical** way of knowing encompasses moral knowledge as well as how ethical choices fit within the legal parameters. It is working together for a common purpose or good. One is unable to predict the outcome of the complex choices made available within contemporary health care. What are the rules? Within the ethical context, can there be rules aside from moral reasoning?

Developing Spirituality

We develop awareness by tapping into the modes of our consciousness. In the spirituality class I coteach, learning strategies help students move spirituality from the abstract to the practical. Challenging our awareness through the various ways of knowing ourselves, we can choose a sense of direction. It is by knowing our direction, where we intend to go or be, that we can act consistently in times of crisis. We can act in truth with our values.

An example is the emergency response of health care providers when a patient experiences cardiac arrest. A caregiver who is in tune with his/her own sense of values, will remember the person for whom the technology is brought into use. It may be a squeeze of the hand, brief eye contact or a call by name. A caregiver acting from authenticity will act competently from the left-brain knowing to a right-brain connection with the patient. Consider the difference of the spirituality of human connection versus a sole reliance on technology. The caregiver ends the emergency with a different feeling or mode of consciousness through the mutuality arising from caring with the heart.

The challenge of interdependence lies in how we manage human relationships. A strategy useful for helping caregivers understand our human interconnectedness involves a ball of string or cord. Holding the end of the string, the leader tosses the ball of string to one of the group, asking for that person to share one unique statement of who they are. That person, in turn, tosses the ball of string to another group member, asking the same question while holding onto the string. When all members of the group have similarly been included, the entire group stands, holding up their place in the unwound interconnected string. The crisscrossing string is a visual reminder of our interdependence. Answers to questions about who we are illustrates our diversity. Recognition of individual uniqueness adds to a sense of value. Holding onto a piece of the string reinforces the essential role each of us has in our relationships.

Movies offer a common experience for encouraging group discussion on observations of spirituality in the world. Students in the spirituality class are given the pleasant assignment of viewing a movie and completing a brief study guide (Table 1) identifying the spiritual needs of the central character. The plot is analyzed in terms of how these needs were expressed within the resolution of the story's values. Through small group discussions, students explore applications of spiritual resolutions within their own experience.

Table 1

STUDY GUIDE

The purpose of this assignment is to observe spiritual needs in everyday life and examine ways others seek resolution of those needs. You are to watch a commercial movie in which a central character is faced with significant choices related to spiritual needs. Please answer the following as a study guide.

Name of movie: _____

Central theme: _____

Main character: _____

Major spiritual needs: _____

_____

_____

How were these issues resolved? _____

_____

_____

What are principles you can apply to your life? _____

_____

_____

An example is in the defining moment in the movie, *Nobody's Fool.* Paul Newman, as the aging worker whose life seems a series of wrong decisions, recognizes his essential contribution to his small circle of relationships. The change in his demeanor following this poignant enlightenment forms the core of his being as he reconciles his meaning and purpose for his remaining years.

Exercising this mode of awareness often results in a shift of priorities by bringing our values and our actions into alignment. This reconciliation of who we are as authentic beings delivers the satisfaction necessary for harmonious living. It brings us in touch with the core of our being, our caring from the heart.

Boykin and Schoenhofer (1995) and Parker (1994) have developed specific teaching modalities based on aesthetic ways of knowing (Carper 1978). The shared reflection of an artist's rendering, the baring of soul regardless of medium, helps us reach inside to stir a response from our own experience. We explore who we are as we reflect in the vision of another.

An exercise in the healing art of clay helps students realize how one's innermost self expresses itself in outward manifestations (Parker, 1994). Each student is given a piece of potter's clay. The session begins with quiet music selected for its healing nature while the facilitator leads the students in centering, relaxing, and focusing on their inner being. Working the clay with their fingers, the warmth of the body softens it, making it malleable and responsive to the maker. As organic matter, the clay begins to show its life; and, as each participant yields to his/her soul, a shape is rendered. Quiet conversation begins and students begin to voice their response to the experience and the meaning of their own clay form.

As caregivers, we emphasize all forms of communication. This work with clay and other aesthetic learning strategies help students understand the impact of nonverbal communication. The unspoken tension of the body carries a message which the power of the clay illustrates in a tactile way.

Creativity is an important aspect of self-awareness in developing spirituality. The freedom of expression records one's reactions, thoughts and feelings formed by the intensity of relationships. Through creative expression we are able to share the story of our experiences, creating connections through the sharing (Chinn & Watson, 1994). The instructor must constantly be thinking of new sources of learning strategies: literature (literary introspection), case study, creative writing, story, journalling, meditation, clay, discovery, brainstorming, conflict resolution, negotiation—all approaches that allow a close and systematic observation of one's own experience.

To illustrate her theory of human caring, Watson (1990) uses a new language in her more recent work, one of metaphor and poetry, to communicate, convey and elucidate human caring and healing. Literature is a useful way to portray integration of the soul in holistic health care.

Boyd (1988) discusses phenomenology as interactive learning which increases awareness of lived experiences. Dialogue is a way to understand the duality of being/doing in nursing. Students and faculty often express their response to caregiving through creative and reflective writings. An example is "Connecting," written by an oncology nurse reflecting on care of cancer patients (Headley, 1995):

> *Caring,*
> *For women who suffer like me and like you*
> *The essence of that which I do*
> *   to ease the agony and the pain*
> *When cure can no longer be gained.*
>
> *Sharing,*
> *My heart aches to aid*
> *The women who have paid*
> *With body, strength and soul*
> *   to abate this senseless rage.*
>
> *Bearing,*
> *The news of death and defeat*
> *How my sadness pours free*
> *   and how my eyes weep*
> *As I carry their sorrow inside of me.*
>
> *Yet,*
> *From tender moments of caring*
> *   for withered bodies, no longer whole*

Comes a shared sense of peace
And the touching of our souls.

Using a wider variety of modes of awareness can help to interpret realities of lived experience. Expanding the use of the
humanities, art and music in the caregiving process expands
awareness and interacts with the healing process (Dossey, et al.,
1995). Analytical skills can be used in interpreting story and
applying to health care. The use of prose in logs, case studies,
anecdotes, dialogue, fictional and autobiographical accounts of
experience, response to art, and artistic expression are learning
strategies to fit the '90s consciousness (Young-Mason, 1995).
Such strategies lead us to attend to our internal selves as well as
our interior selves.

Reconciliation of Values

Life is a journey of interdependence. We live best when we
live relationally. Knowing the source of our meaning and purpose enables us to live life according to our basic value systems.
To be able to live consistently, we need to forge our own mission
statements of what life is about. Adapted from Covey (1990), a
process for assessing one's values, roles, significant others and
expectations is shown in Table 2. Completion of this exercise
leads to a draft of a mission statement, or philosophy, to record
how one wants to live life. As an exercise for students, this
process allows an understanding of the inner conflicts of com-
peting roles and expectations, of values which do not match
one's roles, and of realizing one's mortality. Living by a mission
statement reminds us of the interdependence which enables us
to develop and grow to maturity. It is through our relationships
we uncover new meanings and embrace our fundamental values.

Table 2

PERSONAL MISSION STATEMENT

ADAPTED FROM

STEPHEN COVEY'S
SEVEN HABITS OF HIGHLY SUCCESSFUL PEOPLE

A personal mission statement can be a powerful tool in providing direction and meaning to your life. The strength of a personal mission statement is threefold:

a. Writing a personal mission statement encourages you to think deeply about your life. It causes you to expand your perspective and to examine your innermost thoughts and feelings. In this process, you clarify what is really important to you.

b. Writing the statement imprints self-selected values and purposes firmly in mind. They can then become part of the "software of your head" in providing direction and a sense of commitment to values you have committed to follow.

c. Connecting the mission to daily and weekly plans enables you to obtain direct, immediate benefit from this document, which keeps your personal vision alive throughout everyday life.

d. The process of writing a mission statement involves as much *discovery* as it does *creation,* as you become more aware of natural talents and tendencies that you've always possessed. Don't rush the process; rather, take whatever time you require and think deeply about the questions that follow.

1. INFLUENTIAL PERSON

a. Who has affected your life in a significant way for good? Identify one person who has exerted (knowingly or unknowingly) a positive influence in your life.

_____

b. List the qualities you most admire in this person.

_____

c. What qualities did you gain from this person?

_____

2. DEFINING WHO YOU WANT TO BECOME

It's relatively easy to define the things we want to have (possessions, money) and what we want to do (experiences, travel, etc.), but an inside-out approach to life begins with a definition of what we'd like to be (qualities of character). The next three questions should serve to clarify your thinking in each of these areas. Legitimate power in our lives always originates with the **bes.**

a. What I want to have (possess):

_____

b. What I want to do (experience):

_____

c. What I want to be (qualities of character):

_____

3. DEFINING YOUR LIFE ROLES

You live your life in roles—not in the sense of role-playing but in authentic categories of life you have chosen to implement. You may have roles in work, family, and community organizations, as well as in other areas of your life. These roles can provide a natural framework in helping you to define what you want to be. You may choose to define your various roles in any way you wish.

Examples of roles being filled by one person: *Wife/Mother; Student; Task Force Member; Strategic Planner; PTA Board Member; Friend*

Write your roles on a separate page. Next, identify a key person related to each role. Then project yourself forward in time toward the end of your life and write a brief statement describing this person's feelings and thoughts **as you would want to be described** in that particular role.

	Roles	Key Person	How I Want to Be Described
a.			
b.			
c.			
d.			
e.			

4. WRITE A DRAFT OF YOUR PERSONAL MISSION STATEMENT

When you feel you have an accurate idea of how your roles contribute to the quality of character you'd like to strengthen or acquire, write your personal mission statement.

Spiritual Assessment

Sullender (1988) identifies five basic human spiritual needs, including: meaning and purpose, a sense of mystery, sacredness and wonder of a deity, a sense of trust, and hope in time of hardship. Each of us struggles with these five basic issues of life, moving at various times of our development and journeys in search of their significance in our lives.

1. Meaning and purpose: Humans ask "why," wanting to know the meaning of events in determining that life has a meaningful purpose.
2. Mystery, sacredness, wonder of the deity: The universal need to connect with the mysterious other leads us to want to know the impenetrable exists. One's encounter with the holy other is at the center of every religion. That sense of wonder has diminished with the marvels of the technological age, sometimes leaving an emptiness from the lack of connection.
3. Self-acceptance: Self-criticism is at the root of so many illnesses. We tend to project our self-dislike onto others, giving evidence of the development of prejudice. Each of us must come to terms with our own mistakes and setbacks. Forgiveness is a major part of every religion and is a cornerstone to self-acceptance. As one accepts oneself, one is able to love and give to the other, a hallmark for therapeutic caregiving.
4. Sense of trust: Trust is the cornerstone of personality development that provides the foundation for dealing with crises. AS one surrenders control, one increases power. It is the trust in the deity that gives rise to hope, necessary for sustained, fruitful living.
5. Hope: Living with hope in time of hardship offers the expectation of goal attainment. It is the expectation of the future that largely determines that future. The psychology of hope gives one options; lack of hope reduces the options. Hope allows one to trust in something beyond the present reality.

To begin to understand the soul of the other, a series of open-ended questions evolving from the five spiritual needs can serve as the basis of a spiritual assessment (Table 3). Other more detailed assessments are recorded in nursing and pastoral care literature (Carpenito, 1993; Carson, 1989; Stoll, 1984). Reflecting on these questions can stimulate exploration into one's purpose and meaning (Starck, 1992), helping define the spiritual self. Answers may show the need for referral to those skilled in the art of spiritual intervention.

Table 3

SPIRITUAL ASSESSMENT

1. How do you describe your philosophy of life?
2. How do you describe the meaning in your life?
3. How is the state of your health impacting your family? Your situation? Your life? What bothers you the most about being ill?
4. What are your sources of help? Who are the most important people in your life? To whom do you turn when in need?
5. What is the role of religion in your life? What religious practices are meaningful to you?
6. How do you describe your needs right now? How may we help?

Spiritual well-being is synonymous with harmony and interconnection of relationships. These relationships cover a broad spectrum and can be either time or person related. The way one relates to an ultimate other, regardless of the way one may define the deity or creator, is a significant interconnection. Expressions of mutual love and concern are found in connections with others. The harmony of valuing one's inner self shows itself in reduced anxiety. From past relationships we recognize the influence of sociocultural and religious practices. Meaning and purpose arise from out of the present, and the future offers the hope of ultimate integration. Inner harmony results from a strong sense of satisfaction with self and life (Carson, 1989), giving validation to one's spirituality.

Living an Integrated Life

How does a strong sense of spirituality influence the way one lives within the professional world? Bolman and Deal (1995) offer an excellent guide in their proposed theory of leadership and the meaning of life. At the core of their message is the recognition that true leadership arises from the heart of the leader. Through the search for the soul, one learns the value of the four gifts of leadership which emerge from two dualities: yin and yang, matter and spirit. Opposites that make each other possible through a balance providing harmony, these gifts are love, power, authorship and significance.

From yin, caring and compassion offer the gift of *love.* Yang relates to autonomy and influence, expressed through the gift of *power.* The pragmatic world is represented by matter, the gift of *authorship,* which includes accomplishment and craftsmanship. In putting your own signature on your work, the sheer joy of creating something of lasting value, is the spirit, the soul of life. The gift of *significance* is the feeling of adding something special to the world.

In discovering the soul, we find the way to life, living in relationship and humanity, knowing our place in the universe. Renewal comes from knowing our work is significant, that we make a difference in the world. As caregivers, caring from the heart epitomizes a life of significance, directed by a harmonious inner self.

REFERENCES

Bolman and Deal, T. (1994). *Leading with soul.* San Francisco: Jossey-Bass.

Boyd, C. O. (1988). Phenomenology: A foundation for nursing curriculum. In *Curriculum revolution: Mandate for change* (pp. 65–88). New York: National League for Nursing.

Boykin, A. and Schoenhofer, S. (1993). *Nursing as caring: A model for transforming practice.* New York: National League for Nursing Press.

Carpenito, L. J. (1993). *Nursing diagnosis: Application to clinical practice.* Philadelphia: J. B. Lippincott.

Carper, B. (1978). Fundamental powers of knowing in nursing. *Advances in Nursing Science,* 13–23.

Carson, V. (1989). *Spiritual dimensions of nursing practice.* Philadelphia: W. B. Saunders.

Chinn, P. L. and Watson, J. (Eds.) (1994). *Art and aesthetics in nursing.* New York: National League for Nursing.

Covey, S. (1990). *The seven habits of highly effective people.* New York: Simon and Schuster.

Dossey, B., Keegan, L., Guzetta, C., Kolkeimer, L. (1995). *Holistic nursing: A handbook for practice.* Albany, N.Y.: Delmar

Fitchett, G. (1993). *Assessing spiritual needs: A guide for caregivers.* Minneapolis: Augsburg.

Frankl, V. (1959). *Man's search for meaning.* New York: Beacon.

Gaut, D. (1986). Evaluating caring competencies in practice. *Topics in Clinical Nursing,* 8(2), 77–83.

Headley, J. (1995). *Connecting.* Unpublished prose used with permission, The University of Texas Health Science Center at Houston.

Keegan, L. (1994). *The nurse as healer.* Albany, N.Y.: Delmar.

Parker, M. (1994). The healing art of clay. In D. Gaut and A. Boykin (Eds.), *Caring as healing: Renewal through hope.* New York: National League for Nursing.

Roach, M. S. (1992). *The human act of caring: A blueprint for the health professions* (Rev. ed.). Ottawa: Canadian Hospital Association Press.

Sherwood, G. (1992). The caregiver's response to the experience of suffering. In P. Starck and J. McGovern (Eds.), *Human suffering: An invisible dimension of illness.* New York: National League for Nursing.

———. (1995). The chemistry of nurses' caring: A model for humane health care. *Humane Medicine: A Journal of the Art and Science of Medicine,* 11(2), 62–65.

Starck, P. (1992). The human spirit: The search for meaning and purpose through suffering. *Humane Medicine: A Journal of the Art and Science of Medicine,* 8(2), 132–37.

Stiles, M. K. (1990). The shining stranger: Nurse-family spiritual relationship. *Cancer Nursing,* 13(4), 235-45.

Stoll, R. I. (1984). Spiritual assessment: A nursing perspective. In R. Fehring (Ed.), *Proceedings of the conference on spirituality.* Milwaukee: Marquette University.

Sullender, S. (1988). *Grief and Growth: Pastoral resources for emotional and spiritual growth.* Mahwah, N.J.: Paulist Press.

Watson, J. (1988). *Nursing: Human science and human care–a theory of nursing.* New York: National League for Nursing.

———. (1990). Transpersonal caring: A transcendent view of person, health, and healing. In M. Parker (Ed.), *Nursing theories in practice.* New York: National League for Nursing.

Young-Mason, J. (1995). *States of exile: Correspondences between art, literature, and nursing.* New York: National League for Nursing.